Sinners Have Souls Too

MaeDeans

xulon PRESS

DuBOIS

Table of Contents

Special Thanks

S pecial gratitude and love goes to my husband who I know is a gift from God. In loving him, I realize what is more important is to LOVE the giver of the gift. Thanks to my children whom I love dearly. In spite of my unchaste past, they listen to my instructions about having an abundant life, have grown up to face the challenges of life with God as their personal Savior, become productive citizens and God fearing parents. Also, to my parents who lived an exemplary Christian life (My mother crossed over, December 31, 2002 and my father joined her on, January 25, 2004). Finally, I give God all the Glory for the things He has done for me, a sinner who has been saved by His forgiving grace.

MaeDeans

Preface

This book is nothing more than reported experience with spiritual conviction. As my early years passed the scripture John 3:16, *"For God so loved the world that he gave His one and only son, that whosoever believes in Him shall not perish, but have eternal life"* (NIV) became an inconceivable promise. Wickedness took preeminence in my life. I was so destructive, it is a wonder that God would save me, and even if I could have a little hope in believing in these profound words the question was still how could I let Him save me? I had become too wicked.

The characters' names in this book have been changed to protect the identity of the people involved and also because they convey no real meaning. Only the memories, being transparent in the transition to spiritual awakening will remain impressively on one's mind. The level of your carnality will determine how this book will affect you. In spite of some sordid experiences that took place, God's mercy was always present. Realizing God rains on the just and the unjust, it is His wish that no one be lost in the clutches of demonic power.

"For the Son of Man (Jesus) came to save those which are lost." Matthew 18:11, (KJV)

I'm writing this book as a Spirit-filled Christian. I have come a long way to the realization that without God, you can do nothing of yourself, not to speak of the peace that is acquired through salvation. After reading these pages, I trust that this total experience will encourage you to trust in God and His promises as expressed in the Word of God for your salvation. You will surely know for yourself that the power of God is unspeakable in its abounding love. These pages of my true-life experiences will convince you of that. Reference the scriptures throughout this book, for it will become truth to you.

Please allow yourself to be open-minded while reading each page. See yourself, if at all possible, and relate this story to your own experiences, learning that salvation is personal.

"You can get rid of all moral filth and the evil that is so prevalent and humbly accept the Word of God that is planted in you, which can save you. Anyone who listens to God's

Word but does not do what it says is like a man who looks at his face in the mirror and after looking at himself, goes away and immediately forgets what he looks like."
James 1:21, 23-24(NIV)

True salvation portrays the very essence of happiness, peace, and joy that must be shared. You, who have ears, listen to these words and embrace the salvation of the Lord. I have seen how God has saved other wretched sinners from lives of sin. I believe that through the grace of the Lord Jesus Christ anyone can be saved, for He saved me.

CHAPTER ONE

No Pain, No Gain

Whenever you seem depressed or in those times when you want to praise God for his goodness, all you have to do is to let your mind travel back in time, remembering from whence you came. Even if you are not a born again Christian, you can't help to think about how God has kept you. God has given you reasonably good health; allowed you to attain comfortable prosperity; and a portion of happiness, while stepping-up the ladder of self-achievement. One's memory is precious in recognizing the keeping power of God. Think of how He has protected you in spite of your sinful nature. It's a wonder how God, through His spirit, constantly sought to save my rebellious sick soul from sin.

I was born into a Christian family and had a proper upbringing, but at an early age I began to rebel against what I knew was right in the sight of God. Because I could not see God to recognize Him, I searched for the almighty joy and happiness I needed in men, beginning with my father. I have been told that this is supposed to have been the beginning of all my problematic behaviors and attitudes. But, with the most professional analysis and the influence of our environment as a factor, you cannot ignore the sinful nature of man, which dominates our lives.

> *"We all like sheep, have gone astray; each of us has turned to our own way."* Isaiah. 53:6a. as *"we all have sinned and fallen short of the glory of God."* Romans 3:23 (NIV-rev.)

Most of the time the battle is with ourselves, especially when we have been exposed to the truth of God's word. Your conscience makes you aware of the choices you make between doing what is right as opposed to that which could be detrimental to your well being.

> We become prey to our own wickedness, as do false prophets. *"The Lord knows how to deliver the Godly out of temptation, and to reserve the unjust to the Day of Judgment, to be punished. There are those of us who walk after the flesh in the lust of uncleanness, self willed and not afraid to speak evil of anyone. Even having eyes full of adultery, and cannot cease from sinning, enticing your peers, exercising covetous practices, cursing your*

*children, forsaking the right way and gone
astray, loving the ways of the unrighteous-
ness."* II Peter 2:9-12, 14 (KJV-rev.)

In my early childhood, the male image became my idol.
As the years passed, I refused to believe that God could
possibly contribute to my contentment and happiness. God
did not have lips to kiss me, arms to hold me, and a body to
love me.

How wrong I have been, for the Bible states
*"Delight yourself in the Lord, and He shall
give you the desires of your heart."* Psalms
37:4 (NIV)

*"God will keep you in perfect peace, whose
mind is stayed on Him."* Isaiah 26:3a (KJV)

I felt then, God could only give me that man who could be
the joy of my life, nothing more. Where did these feelings
come from? Was I starved for attention? Was my home life
such that rejection or an atmosphere of boredom caused me
to stray from my upbringing? Whatever happened to develop
this attitude doesn't really matter, for I now know without
God's tender mercy to protect me and finally touch my heart,
sin would have continued to engulf my very existence. All I
can do is to open my life memories to you, and possibly you
can assess what psychological reasons influenced my daily

conduct, attitude and lifestyle. You can draw your own opin-
ion. I cannot deny the fact that sin (to willfully lower your
morals standards, removing self from the association of God
and His Laws) ran its course, making me do things I would
not ordinarily do.

> *"It is no more I that do it, but sin that dwells*
> *in me. For I know that in my flesh dwells no*
> *good thing; for to will is present in me; but*
> *how to perform that which is good I find not.*
> *For the good that I would, I did not; but the*
> *evil which I would not, that I did."* Romans
> 7:17-19 (KJV)

I was the oldest child in a household of six children. I
enjoyed being first and often when we were at odds with
each other I used to tell my siblings that I was their stepsis-
ter, a daughter from my father's previous marriage.
Looking much like my father, the statement seemed logical
to the others and I made them believe I was special. At a
very young age, I considered myself special and different
from my immediate surroundings. Because of my long
straight hair, a school nurse would brush my hair instead of
using the metal comb that other students had to endure. I
was not allowed to stand in the corner when I disrupted the
class, for the nurse came to rescue me every time. My art
talent, which won me a scholarship as a child to the local
Art Institute, and being one of the three most intelligent

students in my class, heightened my self-esteem. Even at home I got the attention I needed, mostly because I had severe headaches. I remember the throbbing pains in my head beating like a big bass drum. Breathing or even blinking my eyes was painful. Many times I could not go to school for an entire week. Whether it was poverty or ignorance in which to label the blame, I never got the medical attention I needed for my headaches. I just suffered. Then too, the county hospital was not the place to go for headaches. Only dripping blood, fever over 105 degrees or no evidence of a pulse was the condition that warranted immediate attention. Therefore, pain became my constant companion.

At the age of ten, my importance was rising to its peak because my mother became ill for many months. My complaints were laid aside in order to take over the responsibilities of being the mother of the house, caring for my sisters and brothers. I found pleasure in taking over mother's responsibilities, learning about housekeeping from my daddy, including cooking. Having Christian parents, I had great admiration for them. But having a good looking, hard working father all to myself developed pride in me. He became my hero, a man who could do anything, a perfect man. He was my own little god. I was so caught up that when we crossed the street and he held my hand for safety, I actually wanted people to think we were boyfriend and girlfriend. I loved my mother, but I worshipped my daddy.

"You shall have no other gods before me."
Exodus 20:3 (NIV)

I sought most of my attention and approval from adults as I had little to do with my peers, except for one girlfriend. I had a cousin, eight years my senior, who would visit from out of town. She lived a permissive and what seemed like an exciting life with several lovers; in a motorcycle gang and full of adventures. She was my secret idol. While my mother was disappointed about her lifestyle, I found her exciting especially since she gave me some of her clothes and took me shopping. By the way, she eventually came to herself and now she is a Christian and a spiritual leader in her church. She attended the very church our grandmother worshipped at some eighty years ago.

Jesus speaks of a woman who had lived a wretched life. *"I say unto you, Her sins, which were many, are forgiven; for she loved much; but to whom little is forgiven, the same loves little."* Luke 7:47 (KJV)

Being confined to the house most of the time, due to my illness or my mother's illness, did not make allowance for developing a normal relationship with children my own age. As I grew older, my hips and my back began to give way to pain. I realized this after I became involved in physical sports. My body began to succumb to excruciating pain. I would hide or sit some place quietly for long periods of time waiting for the pain to subside. I did not want to give up those moments of pleasure I received in participating in sports for this was the only time my parents granted me permission to leave from the house for hours at a time. Sometimes in my solitude, I would entertain myself with beautiful fantasies of a healthy and loving life.

My teenage years were greatly altered from that of most teenagers. To begin with, my father's attention towards me began ebbing away from me and flowing to my brothers. They were growing older and now able to be his running buddies. Besides the feeling of rejection from my father, I knew my health was growing worse.

When taking a physical examination to enter high school, the prognosis gave reason to believe I had polio, like my younger brother. I was admitted into the hospital immediately and assigned to an adult ward because the children's ward was full. Again, I was cut off from my peers. During my early years in high school there was an awards program for academic achievements and I was receiving one. I was in so much pain that as I proceeded across the stage between the throbbing pains from my monthly cramps, I could only get to where the principal was standing and then fell to my knees. I couldn't make another step. My new white-felt skirt, that had a poodle on a chain on it, was surely damaged more so than my ego.

For a period of almost two years, I was constantly in and out of the hospital having X-rays, bed rest, X-rays, physical therapy, X-rays, special diets, more X-rays and consultations in front of an audience of doctors who were trying scientifically to determine my destiny. The medical profession could not understand how I was walking, yet feared that in trying to correct the prevalent deformity, there could be a chance that paralysis might occur. I was on a special high protein and calcium diet. I was ordered to drink a gallon of milk, including malted milk shakes and medium rare steaks daily. Because we were poor, the members from our church constantly contributed to our family needs. I was to eat calf liver, which I hated. So they bottled the meat in ginger ale to extract the blood. I managed to drink it only because it tasted like soda pop.

While I was confined in the orthopedic ward, the question of my suffering seemed irrelevant. I saw others in so much more pain. Some of them in full body casts lay helpless, unable to attend to their own needs. Some had to remain that way for as long as two years. Medical technology has certainly improved since the late fifties. I made myself available to those patients, helping and serving them with an air of professionalism like a nurse.

"I was like prophets who spoke in the name of the Lord, they suffered affliction and patience like that of Job, and was counted happy which endure for the Lord is of tender mercy." James 5:11(KJV-rev.)

I never thought of myself as a crippled teenager, but as a capable, highly intelligent, caring young woman. Of course, I often helped myself to their unwanted oatmeal served often at breakfast and their beans for supper, a specialty of the County Hospital. I had tutors while at home and when I was hospitalized. When I was able to attend school, I was placed in a room outside the principal's office. All my teachers had to come to me regarding school assignments, because I was to do as little walking or stair climbing as possible. No one took into consideration I walked ten city blocks to and from school. I still managed to remain on the honor roll until I had to drop out after an altercation with one of my teachers, whom I slapped. I still had frequent hospital visits. Everyone was mystified as to how I was still able to walk, even though I was constantly in pain. I was given crutches to assist me. Those times when I was alone, many times in pain, I would ask God to take the pain away. All the while, I constantly looked for ways to handle my everyday activities, focusing on how I could walk. I swayed my hips to minimize my discomfort and to conceal my limp, especially when I got tired.

King David cried out like I so often have done. *"Have mercy on me, O lord, for I am weak; O Lord heal me, for my bones are irritated (both my body and soul)."* Psalms 6:2 (KJV-rev.)

One day when I was alone, a young man who went to my church came to visit me. He made an attempt to molest me. Using the crutches I drove him from my home, only to realize the pain I had become accustomed to was not present. In fact, to this day unless I over extend myself, I'm free from pain. Yes, the deformity is there but the pain is all but gone. As a result, I was finally discharged from the doctor's care at the age of seventeen. I did not realize I was healed.

Yes, I was born to a lower middle class family as society dictates, with a dreaded disease that could have visibly crippled me for life. Yet, the God who made me allowed experiences in my childhood to help develop endurance, unselfish love, faith, long-suffering determination and even dependence on Him at an early age. I felt my self-worth. Sometimes our childhood is not the way we want it or expect. Things happen, people change, and you change. But whatever happens, the experiences help to make us. My soul's will, desire and emotions were being developed. The choices I made or will be making, especially my desire to be loved consumed me. I did not want to let go of the love my father showed me, making me feel special and necessary. I didn't realize the God who made me had always loved me.

CHAPTER 2

Where Did All My Youth Go?

I felt I adjusted well in an active sense. I was always trying to participate in the things teenagers usually did while still feeling that I didn't belong. I had my own personal thoughts, for my friends were limited. The lack of having someone to communicate with caused me to lapse into long periods of daydreaming. I knew nothing about the evil and the temptation that lurks like a thief who watches a house, waiting for an opportune time to break-in and steal what does not belong to him; or like a lion who stalks the jungle to see whom he may destroy.

> *"Be self-controlled and alert. Your enemy the devil prowls around like a roaring lion, looking for someone to devour."* I Peter 5:8 (NIV)

Some would say I was completely out of touch with

reality. I had no peer group to identify with. I felt I was too old to be my father's pal and yet could not ignore the excitement that I craved. Due to my physical condition I was different, so I began to fill my life with the idea that I was already grown-up. Who needs the years between the ages of 13 and 16? Everyone seemed so immature. Because of my attitude about myself, adult men gradually drew my interest and attention. My strict upbringing may have influenced my willingness to do just about anything I was told not to do. Everything outside my home and church seemed exciting. These worldly people seemed laidback, carefree, and had happy-go-lucky spirits. Everyone seemed to be having a good time. They just did what felt good. I was ignorant to life. I felt secure in my adult surroundings, especially since my training was reinforced by the fact it was unlawful for an adult to take advantage of a minor. So, I felt safe. However, worldliness breathed an air of excitement.

The neighbors around my house always seemed to be having a grand time, while my home had an air of reverence. The music, especially blues, the gambling, drinking, and the verbal commotions intrigued me. I have to admit, I knew very little about anything. To add to the mystery of the world out there, I had to sneak around. There was no way on earth my parents would condone those things I thought I had to be a part of. It became a battle between being good and seeking adventure. I preferred the excitement of what evil presented. You must understand, I did not think of it as sin, just exciting. Maybe my parents would not understand, but I felt that I was not bothering anyone.

I ventured out, getting into narrow escapes and situations that could have resulted in disastrous outcomes. I was in the clutches of grown men with lustful desires. One particular time, I visited the home of one of my adult admirer's relatives. His aunt and uncle, along with a few friends were drinking and clowning around. They began teasing my friend because he had not had sex with me. He was drunk off of beer, and gave way to the intimidation. Someone in the household who was shaving came out of the bathroom, laying the razor down on a nearby end table and joined in on the taunting. My so-called boyfriend began grabbing me, trying to force himself on me. During the scuffle, I slipped and fell and he climbed on top of me. I panicked and somehow grabbed the razor, which had fallen from the table. I found out later or realized I had cut his throat, not very deep, from ear to ear. Being full of blood, I broke free and ran to my girlfriend's house where she helped me to clean up. My parents never found out. I remember some weeks later, when I saw him again he still had bandages on his neck. The ordeal resulted in him having a bad scar. Even with that frightening experience, I had no fear of being abused.

I knew little about danger. I was naive. A supposed friend promised me that he would help sell all of the raffle tickets I was selling for a school project if I met him at his job. Retrieving used pop-bottles, I got enough money to get where I was going miles away from home via a bus. Mind you, I was sneaking, something I became good at. In fact, it was the first time I went anywhere alone. That night I met a male associate named Joseph who prevented a group of men from raping me. This was a situation that could have been avoided if I had enough sense to carry bus fare with me in order to return home from my destination. Joseph, I found out, was a small time hustler even though he worked two legitimate jobs. He was tall and strong in stature. He had several lady friends who would do most anything for him. He had impressive cars, had a good line of conversation, and was respected and feared by his peers. It was one of his employee's who lured me to a garage that stored cars on a promise that he and his friends would buy all my raffle tickets. As I entered, several men approached me. Within a few seconds, Joseph walked in on the scuffle that was taking place with me in one of the back seats of a new car. He disbanded them and threatened to fire them all. From that point, he became my idol and savior. He was someone who could be like a father, as my protector and a man of passion.

Every chance I got; I went to one of his jobs, asking questions about life and relationships with men. However, he was short on words. He seemed to have done and knew about almost everything. I got very emotionally involved, making believe I was grown even though I was only fifteen years of age. I found out where he lived and would catch a bus and visit unannounced, often interfering with his agenda. One day on an unexpected visit from me, he was still in bed. As usual he would just let me in and continue to do whatever he was doing. I tried to get his attention, even tried to seduce him by climbing into his bed and kissing him on his face. But I got no reaction from him, nor would I have known what to do if he had reacted. He loved his jewelry, which I grabbed that day, because I was being ignored. I ran out of his apartment with him in hot pursuit in his underclothes and bare feet. He snatched me up off my feet, returned back to his apartment, tied me to a chair and got back into bed. I wanted to scream but I knew I was in just as much trouble as he would be, so I just begged him to let me go. When he got me under control, he called my mother asking her to keep me away from him because I was a child who didn't have any idea what I was doing. Of course I was put on punishment. That was the last time I saw him until I was twenty-one. When I saw him come into a store where I was working, we renewed our friendship, which lasted over six years until he had to relocate. The truth of the matter is, while he never took advantage of me he shared wisdom about the street, especially how men think and react to women. There were a few of things that stuck with me: do not let anything negative control you; men want what they think they cannot have; remember, a man wants it and you got it, so play hard and don't give in. These words of wisdom are like the advice that my father had mentioned. He said, "Do not want someone who don't want you," which I attributed to helping me to make some good choices in life. It helped sustain me.

I was not allowed to go to parties. So, I would walk

down the street at night when I was supposed to be in front of my house, playing hide and seek. Of course, no one ever found my best friend or me. We would stroll past taverns, peep in and dance on their doorsteps until someone would request that we leave. Dancing was not the real attraction. It was the lyrics to songs like "Release Me" by Esther Phillips, "God Bless the Child" by Billy Holiday and "It's Hurts Me Too" by Little Miss Cornshuck that intrigued me. Those words of feeling, I could identify with even at an early age. I shared none of my feelings with anyone and daydreamed about the excitement of living in a world of gaiety, adventure, and mystery of the unknown. I secretly desired to live a life that my parents surely wouldn't approve of. I was sure I could handle any situation like I mastered my physical pain.

While I was dealing with my bout with polio, I was shuffled from home to the hospital with group conferences and extensive examinations, starting all over again at each stay in the hospital. During one of my stays at the hospital, at the age of fifteen, I met George who also had polio. He was confined to a wheelchair at that time. He was playing the piano in the hospital's chapel as I was passing by. When he spoke, his voice was gentle and caring and I felt he could not harm me. During his stay he wrote me poems, sent me flowers and played love songs for me. I was a young teenager and he was a young man who I believed would not be of any threat. I felt secure because he would not or could not desert me. His showing of respect toward me would have pleased my mother. I was being treated like a woman. He told me about the nightclubs where he played the piano, even in his condition. I dreamed of going to those same places, but I was crippled by my strict Christian home life. When I returned home from the hospital, I continued to see my new friend. I went to school each day, managing to stay on the honor roll, while sneaking out at night to see him. I would actually wait until my father had left for work and my mother was asleep. Taking carfare, I walked several blocks to take the commuter train, riding it down to one of the corrupt sides of town, not knowing the kind of danger I was in. I exposed myself to the danger of the urban nightlife. Homeless people who gave the train an unpleasant odor, which I was not accustomed to; hustlers, pimps and their unkempt whores; underpaid domestic foreign laborers; derelicts; and thieves rode these trains. After approximately six months, I could not keep up the pace. Between the pains my body was suffering, the lack of sleep and the fear of being caught, I took my life into my own hands. No one needed me at home. My father was too busy working two jobs and my mother had other children to tend too. My mother was not sick anymore. Taking a few clothes, including my new bright red taffeta dress my mother made for me, and my first pair of patent leather heels, I left home and school to go to be with George. I went to him because I felt he cared and needed me.

George lived in a flophouse in the slums where dope, prostitution and killing were normal everyday happenings.

A caged vestibule protected this transit hotel where he stayed. The clerk only let people enter in by permission. Rats and roaches roamed the premises, allowing little thoroughfare for humans not to ignore the musty smell. It was strange surroundings, yet I could not recognize danger. He would not allow me out of his sight nor could I understand George's state of fear because of my presence. George constantly repeated how much trouble I was causing him because of my age. I told him in no uncertain terms, if I had to leave I would kill myself. He let me stay while making plans for us to get married.

After about three months in one 10X11 foot room and having to share one meal, I wanted to live that exciting life I dreamed about. I began to realize that I was still being restricted from freedom.

> *"Having eyes of fornication and cannot cease from sin; enticing unstable souls: an heart they have exercised with covetous practices; cursed children: which have forsaken the right way and gone astray. They speak great swelling words of vanity, they allure through the lust of the flesh, much wants. They promise them liberty, while they themselves are servants of corruption, for of whom man overcome, of the same he is brought in bondage."* II Peter 2:14-15a, 18-19 (KJV)

I literally had to fight to get this freedom. One Easter evening, I wanted to go and see one of my favorite performers that was scheduled to appear in town, with my red dress on. George said I couldn't risk being seen. In an effort to keep me from leaving, we got into a scuffle. The disturbance caused the desk clerk to call the police.

When they arrived and assessed the situation, they summoned the juvenile authorities. I tried to be tough when I was turned over to the delinquency officers. Fear engulfed me for the first time. My mother was very angry and embarrassed. My father showed concern as they watched me from their car while I was ushered to the police car along with my friend. I wanted to say to them how sorry I was, but my pride made me hold my head up high and blink back the tears as they took me away.

My temporary home for juveniles made me know I would not survive. This place housed inmates ranging from poor homeless run-a-ways to killers. I immediately made claim to my physical condition and faked signs of a mental breakdown, which required isolation. I watched and listened to everything around me. In the dormitory areas, lesbians kept many fellow inmates awake at night while they roamed from one bed to another, making advances toward each other. Some girls were forced into compromising situations. There were girls who were so sexually frustrated and confused they actually grinded the walls in passion. One young girl had run away from home after being repeatedly molested by her stepfather who finally was killed by her mother in her presence. She was raped several times while she was in flight. Can you believe it? I had the nerve to run away from a spiritual home and from God's protection.

> *"The end is better than its beginning, and patience is better than pride. Do not be quickly provoked in your spirit, for anger resides in the lap of fools. Consider what God has done."* Ecclesiastes 7: 8-9, 13a (NIV)

While I was confined for about three months, daydreams could no longer fill my days. Only tears and loneliness replaced them. Prayer soon found my lips, for I had nowhere to turn and wanted to go home. I later learned that the man I thought I wanted to spend the rest of my life with was not only a one-hundred fifty dollar a day junkie, but he was wanted for the murder of a previous girlfriend. I learned he had actually sexually molested me without having sexual intercourse. It was a rude awakening of how much danger I really was in, yet no real harm had came to me. It has been said that God protects babies and fools. I was both. I didn't know God, but he knew me and protected me.

> *"She who strays away from her father and hounds her mother is a daughter that causes shame and brings reproach."* Proverb 19:26 (NIV rev.)

What was it? Was it being sheltered from the real world, neglected from daily conversation with my parents to inform me of the wiles of the devil, or never having been told about sexual awareness and failures that I could be faced with if I ventured out of my safety zone. I knew nothing, only my driven need for adventure to satisfy the passionate urges locked up in my body. Back then I never gave any thought that my soul was a vessel for Satan's devises. All I thought about was satisfying my flesh. Flesh made Adam fall from God's covering in the Garden of Eden. Who was I running from when no one was chasing me? Yet, something within made me feel like I wanted more. I knew what I had done was hurtful and shameful. In trying to be brave in accepting the consequences for my actions, this sinner's soul was truly sorry for the predicament I had gotten myself into. Satan had tricked me in believing man's love was happiness. I was soon to find out how wrong I was.

CHAPTER 3

Too Proud To Beg

The embarrassment and guilt that I felt when I eventually came home from the caged dormitory made me become even more private. I was put in the custody of my parents, reporting to a psychiatrist until I became eighteen years of age. To make amends with my parents, I asked God to forgive me for my sins. I truly was sorry for the mess I'd gotten into. I was conscious that God was the reason why no harm came to me. I was truly frightened.

I did not know why, but no one ever questioned my whereabouts or what had happened. I was grateful for that. At church everyone was gentle and kind. At home, no one said a word. Not until many years later did my mother mention that she dared anyone to question me about anything. Everyone respected her demands. I became frightened of the outside world and guilt stricken in my immediate world at home and church. I would daydream about being loved by men, and the possible ventures that could have materialized based on my past experience, then feel guilty for my thoughts. I cried, prayed and read my Bible, yet I felt a void in my life. Every time the phone rang, fear engulfed my very being. I thought George would be calling me to voice his anger and vendetta for causing him to spend many years in prison, or someone else calling to inquire about my tragic past experience. No one called, inquired in person or showed any visible concerns. I had no one to share my experiences or my thoughts with, except for when I chose to share with my therapist on my weekly visit. During my sessions it was determined that my interests in mature men was because of my love for my father, who refocused his attention away from me to my brothers who were growing older. My sense of purpose was abated since my mother was now healthy and I was becoming a young woman. The need I had of being the most important person in my household as daddy's little girl was no longer a reality. Because of running away and an altercation with a teacher, I had to further my high school education in an alternative school.

Aside from going to church and an alternative school for nine hours, four days a week, I did not have much of a life. I learned songs from the Hit Parade magazines and read love stories from magazines like "Bronze Thrill" and "True Confession". I still had the discomfort of pain in my back and hips. The guilt and shame did make me feel it was better to give my heart to God. At least it would please my parents.

I still continued to have swollen glands in my throat area and severe headaches. This bout of illness came at a time when I wanted to be baptized. But because of my physical condition, it was recommended that I shouldn't be exposed to water. A couple of saints prayed that I would improve. That very next morning when I woke up I felt no pain. Until this day, some forty-five years later, I no longer suffer from this condition of swollen glands and sore throat. This was my first experience with God's divine healing power. I was baptized.

> *"If any is sick among you, let them call for the elders of the Church, and anointing them with oil in the name of the Lord and they shall be healed."* James 5:14

After several months of being home, I met Larry through his cousin, both of whom were living together with his aunt down the street from me. He was quiet, soft-spoken and very congenial. In fact, he said nothing about anything. He conformed to all the rules of my home. Possibly his behavior was attributed to the fact he was seven years older than I was. He took me wherever I wanted to go, which was mainly to the drive-in. He did not go to Church nor did he mind if I went. I felt freedom with him for a long time, for he did not interfere with anything I wished to do. The only occasion that Larry showed any concern or jealousy was when another young man, named John, who lived in the neighborhood asked to marry me. John took me to his newly acquired empty apartment building, supposedly to talk about our future. I thought it was strange that there were so many locks on the door. He tried to seduce me while all the time wanting me to consider marrying him. I guess my main objection was that he just did not appeal to me, even though he was nice looking and tall. The entire ordeal lasted half the night. When John was convinced I just was not interested, he finally agreed to take me home. Both my parents and Larry were waiting up for me. Realizing the possibility of losing me, Larry asked me to marry him.

There was no wedding as my mother had originally planned. Larry and I decided to elope. Larry and I got married, having looked up a preacher in the local telephone book. Along with his cousin and her boyfriend as our witnesses, we entered an elderly couple's home via the rear stairs to the second floor. After the short ceremony in the kitchenette apartment, the preacher's wife offered us cookies and milk. This took place three days after my eighteenth birthday; I took the chance at staying out all night, explaining to my parents that I was spending the night with a friend. Our honeymoon consisted of a one-night stay in a local transit hotel that actually caught fire the very next morning, forcing us to leave abruptly. We continued to live at our respective homes for several months, until my father became suspicious of my behavior. My physical appearance took on a drastic change for I was pregnant. When my father thought it was time, he finally told my mother, who had to cancel the formal wedding plans. In its place we had a reception.

In the early months of my marriage I was a perfect wife. After my house was clean I was often bored, since for no apparent reason, I no longer attended Church. One boring evening while I was pregnant with my daughter, I demanded that my husband play cards with me. He showed little interest in doing so. Finally he agreed and began shuffling the cards as I eagerly waited to find out which game we were about to play. The very next moment, the cards were flying up in the air and all around me. In bewilderment, I heard him say "fifty-two pick-ups," and he turned back to watching television. Now I had something to do. I laughed so hard I was rushed to the hospital, threatening to miscarriage. This happened to me again, when I ate an extra large sausage pizza, which caused my stomach to cramp and made me vomit profusely. This was the extent of my excitement.

The day my daughter was born, after being in labor for only two and half hours, was the very day of the baby shower. This only happened because she was born when I was seven and one-half months pregnant. Immediately upon returning home to my well-kept apartment, I celebrated by having one of our frequent house parties. This caused me to have to go back into the hospital due to complications. Having had a daughter was a rewarding and exciting experience for I felt virtuous, healthy, and loved. Being independent and not on intimate terms with my mother, I had little knowledge about childbearing. I mastered the activities of motherhood through trial and error, along with being a perfect housewife. We did for some reason have company often, playing cards and partying until daybreak. I soon found out that Larry liked to drink and did so every day with his friends. I was truly bored. After I married Larry I just gave up on my Christianity. Larry did not care one way or another about Church, so I did not put forth any effort on my part. I just quit going. I turned my back on God whom I personally knew as a healer, a protector and a Savior.

> *"The backslider in heart shall be filled with his own ways. After you have known God, or rather are known of God, how do you again turn to the weak and its elements, desire again to be under bondage."* Proverbs 14:14a; Galatians 4:9 (KJV)

It wasn't long before there was no joy in being married to Larry. As was the case when he was my boyfriend, he was still quiet, soft spoken, and never gave any objections to my whims, just so long as I did not require any response or commitment from him. He found a good steady job, just a few days before we were married and worked the same job, doing the same duties for some thirty-four years without ever taking a personal day off. He never once caused me any concerns regarding his love or feelings for me. Boredom reigned over my life. My idle mind became Satan's workshop.

Being eighteen years old, married and pregnant, I had to complete my high school education in night school, where I finally graduated. After I graduated, I got a job at a major department store working in their customer service section. I started going out in the evening unescorted. By this I mean, that when I first got married, I wouldn't go anywhere without my husband. All my pinned up inhibition was starting to be released. I felt grown-up and smart enough to face what the world had to offer. I tried to justify my actions for my conduct, believing that just so long as I refrained from outside social intimacy my behavior was okay. I believed I was not guilty of infidelity. I did not realize that social intimacy could lead to infidelity. I frequented lounges; danced a lot, and let men try to entice me. I even allowed them to make physical advances towards me. However, I remained faithful to my husband regarding adultery, at least for a while. I tried desperately to express my anxiety to Larry. He never displayed any objections or complained about my restless spirit. There was no one to tell me to stop. It did not take long before both Larry and I realized there was no love on my part and that I most likely married him to escape my guarded lifestyle at my parent's house. His only comment for my actions was that I should do as I pleased so I can get whatever I thought necessary out of my system.

My permissiveness only grew, especially when my husband refused to go out with me along with several of my female friends. Larry actually locked me out the house, telling me to learn to enjoy myself without him. Afterward, I started to keep company with all kinds of men, from every walk of life. They ranged from blues joint musicians to professional men. The very night he locked me out, I met someone. He lived with his mother so I felt safe. Our relationship ended while we were out at a party and I found out he had a drug addiction and that drugs were being used in my presence. My relationships with men would flourish until they demanded more than I was willing to give up. During this period, God had no place in my life. I felt protected by my husband who would love me for better or for worse.

"The Lord protects the simple hearted (fool),
when I was in great need he saved me (from myself)." Psalm 116:6 (NIV)

After four years of marriage and now two children, I became involved with another man. He was tall and strong in stature. He was ever so gentle, loving and kind. There was nothing he could offer me, since he was married and the father of ten living children. With him I felt like a little girl in that no one would dare do me any harm. I met him at a blues joint while hanging out with the girls. When he walked in, some six feet four inches tall, olive skinned, over 200 pounds, slanted eyes on his round face, I was awe struck. I watched him for hours as he interacted and danced with the guests at his table, especially a tall woman sitting next to him. I found out later that she was his wife. I put my name and phone number on a piece of paper and slid it in his pocket as I walked past him while his wife was dancing with someone else.

The very next day he called me and we met. The relationship developed into an explosive affair. We went out several times a week. Mind you, I was still married. Once when I stayed out all night holding my lover's hand, like we were teenagers, I got this strange feeling that someone was watching me. Sure enough, across the street a bus full of passengers of whom my husband was the driver, was watching me. Knowing I got busted, I fell to my knees on the sidewalk with hands up in surrender. He finally pulled off. I quickly rushed home gathered my children up and went over to my parent's house. My husband called later that evening, telling me that I could come back home and that he would not bother me. Neither of us ever brought up the subject.

It wasn't long before my lover's wife found out about me and let me know by using those famous curse words of threat to leave her husband alone. I even met with her on the street so she could emphasize the fact that not only was she married and had ten children (three sets of twins), but she was also pregnant as we spoke. I simply told her she would miscarry and that her issues should not be with me but with her husband. As it was a winter day, we decided to finish our conversation in the local lounge. As soon as the proprietor saw us, he asked us to leave fearing some physical altercation. I made it plain; the affair would end at her husband's request. As it turned out, she fell and lost her baby after having an explosive argument and a one-sided fight with her husband.

I soon found out I was also pregnant with my third child. Excited, I had no fear or concern as to my fate. I did not care. I decided to make my motherhood known to Larry. After he accepted that I was pregnant and the boyfriend was in no position to care for me, he agreed to remain married and to accept all the responsibility regarding the baby, if my friend would stop seeing me. We managed to be together for the last time, the night before my daughter was born at six and one-half months into my pregnancy on New Year's Day. When I got back home that morning I began to go into labor. Everyone in my household was in a drunken sleep, so I had to either call 911 or have the baby at home alone. I had to be taken to the county hospital in a police paddy wagon. Half dressed with only a scratchy army green blanket to cover my cold body, I went alone. I barely made it. I had my daughter in an unsterilized condition in the elevator in the hospital. Because the staff was not ready to receive me I had torn badly, hemorrhaged, caught a fever and laid in the halls like cattle in a box car until I was able to go home five days later.

I never realized some of the consequences that could befall me. It grieved my husband, but he did not say a mumbling word. I saw the hurt in his eyes, but I only gloried in my own want. Just like Larry loved me he would and did love my baby girl. The relationship with my boyfriend proved to be an inconvenient affair and after a few years it was over. My baby's father paid child support, at least for the next seven years; until I informed him he no longer had to do so by my request. He only saw her once when she was three years old. Each realized they looked alike. To this day, she never asked or needed to ask about him. She has a father in Larry.

"Those who walk after the flesh in the lust of uncleanness, presumptuous are they, self-willed, they are not afraid to speak and do evil." II Peter 2:10 (KJV-rev.)

Once again I resumed my reckless lifestyle. I became restless, even after securing a diploma in accounting in a home school course. Despite the excitement I felt in my many episodes with the different men, I felt God was determined to win my heart back to him. Whenever things didn't go my way or trouble arose, I felt that God was trying to get my attention, to weaken me in order to show my need for him. But I refused to surrender. I would cry in anguish and sorrow for release of my troubled soul, but I would not give in to God. "I will come back to you when I'm ready, not when I have no other alternatives. Do you understand God?" I often spoke to Him out loud. "I would rather drink muddy water and sleep in a hollow oak tree before giving my heart to God, because I have no where else to turn." These were the words I spoke when I was drowning in my own sorrows not recognizing the wooing of the Holy Spirit.

"It is the spirit that makes the soul come alive, the flesh profits nothing; the word of God, is life. Therefore, Jesus said that no man could come unto God, except through Him." John 6:63, 65 (KJV-rev.)

My activities got worse as the years passed. Without work and school to occupy my time, boredom started to raise its head again. I was back on the prowl. The more dangerous the affairs with men, the more I seemed intrigued. The wives and the girlfriends had to know of my existence. I took up gambling at the local bookies as an everyday pastime, along with going to the racetracks, sometimes as much as twice a day. I played cards, mostly pinochle in between parties we had on the weekend. On occasion, dope (marijuana) and stolen goods, mainly fur coats, were stored and processed in our apartment (while we were living on the second floor of my parents' home) unbeknownst to my husband. We were even asked to move from one of our apartments because of the excessive noise that we kept up. Worldliness was a merry-go-round in my life. My time was being occupied, yet in my lonely hours I found myself being faced with my unworthiness to be anybody's wife, mother or daughter.

Like my mother's disappointment in what she saw in me, so was God in His anger towards Israel and Judah, His chosen people. He too stressed *"they turned their back to*

me, and not their face; though I taught them,
rising up early and teaching them, yet they
have not taken heed to receive my instruc-
tions." Jeremiah 7:13 (KJV)

Once in my mother's basement, a very strong discussion developed between my mother and me about my lifestyle. My mother said, "I asked God, what have I done so wrong to have a child like you? I am sorry you were ever born." I heard those words and they penetrated deeply for many years. I didn't know I was under conviction for the Spirit was constantly trying to draw me. I never went to church any more, except for weddings and funerals, for God was so close to being the victor. When I occasionally sat listening to the preached word I felt convicted to change my life for the better. I finally convinced myself that if God wanted me to be his disciple, I would come to myself before it was everlasting too late.

But, it was my responsibility to choose to want to change. *"If I would turn from all of my sins that I committed, and keep God's statues, and do that which is lawful and right, I will surely live (in Christ) and shall not die (in sin)."* Ezekiel 18:31 (KJV)

During my ten years of marriage to Larry two of my children died when they were only a few months old. After three years of marriage, our second child, a son, a very quiet, gentle, and smiling son died at five months. One night when he was sleeping in the bed with his cousin he died of crib death, an unknown explanation for the mysterious dying of infants. Usually, early in the morning he would wake up smiling and seem very happy, actually waking us up with gurgling sounds. Even with having been out most of the night, I had awakened before him. When I looked over in to the bed I immediately noticed that his straight light brown hair appeared very curly. I observed him for a few moments. I approached him slowly and made an effort to turn him over on his back. I grabbed him by his hand and realized that his entire body seemed to rise up as if I were turning over a stiff board. Quickly letting him go, I woke my husband to check out what I was trying not to believe. He was dead.

After the initial shock, I accepted what happened as the law-of-averages (knowing God reigns on the just and the unjust, alike). However, I was so distraught I was unable to attend his funeral. But, when a couple of years later I lost another one of my children, a daughter, I felt God was hitting below the belt. I made it known that if God was trying to get my attention this was not the way. He had to do better than that. I declared I would rather die and go to hell before He could make me serve Him. I never realized that God permits things to happen while trying to get our attention, in any way possible. But it is up to us to accept Him in our lives.

The daughter that died was a beautiful gift of a lover who had been childless. I came to believe that God knew my life would be greatly altered if she had lived. The pain and suffering of her existence would crush the heart of those who truly loved me. I was willing to give up my husband, whom I lied too, my other children and family, to run away from the pressure of my daughter's father who was threatening to expose me. Originally, he did not believe he was the father, because he was diagnosed as sterile while in the Navy. He remained nice to me, but just didn't believe he was the father. After her birth, his entire family assured him she had to be his for she looked like them. Once he saw her, he was obsessed with her. He made it plain that he was taking her from me. He had been to my house several times. I had one child by another man while I was still married, so I couldn't tell my husband the truth this time. Her father was determined to take her. He had left his wife and was making arrangements to take her from me. He said, "I could go with him if I wanted to." He was prepared to kidnap his own daughter.

I remember so vividly the night she died. Early that day, I took her to the doctor because she was running a temperature. He gave me a prescription for penicillin. She was very fretful. That night I actually fell asleep holding her, when my sister insisted I put her to bed before I drop her. Something awakened me suddenly in the middle of the night. I rushed to the crib in the next room. After the death of my son, I decided to relocate the crib to another room so I could get some sleep. I felt this was necessary because of the death of my first child. I awoke every time the baby would make a sound. As I approached the crib, I froze. Even from a distance, the stillness, and once again the curly matted hair, was nothing like the silk hair I had brushed earlier. I fell to my knees in agony, waking my oldest daughter, who I restrained from entering the room. I sent her for my sister downstairs, and when she arrived she examined her only to confirm that she was dead. The autopsy revealed that her naval was not completely healed from the inside, setting up infection which eventually poisoned her system at the age of three months. The entire ordeal left me angry with God.

> I was like a strange woman *"which forsook the guidance of her youth, forgot the covenant of her God. For her house inclined unto death and her paths unto the dead."* Proverbs 2:17-18 (KJV-rev.)

Her funeral was stressful because my daughter's father's family was present and they insisted on trying to comfort me. I convinced my husband to return to work the next day, allowing me to bury her alone. I let her father go with me. After we lowered her into the ground, I told him good-bye and did not see him for the next ten years. I saw him at his brother's Church, years later and found out he had remarried, had a daughter and named her after ours. The emotion and memories I felt were not pleasant, so I said good-bye to her father for the last time.

I had truly lost my place in the home and
with God by being rebellious, forgetting that
*"in the house of the righteous is much trea-
sure, but in the revenues of the wicked is
trouble."* Proverbs 15:16 (KJV)

Once again I realized how much deeper I was sinking
into sin. I was becoming like a vulture seeking my prey. I
couldn't control how self-centered and uncompassionate I
was becoming. I only remained sensitive to the children I
had brought into this world. Having mothered them was
the only healthy feeling I had about myself. Even the many
baths with almost scalding water could not wash away my
uncontrollable guilt and gnawing insensitivity. I actually
gloated that I was the devil's angel and took pride in warning my next male victim's. Some people actually
wondered if I was possessed. I still daydreamed, but my
thoughts were perverted and strange. Even my dreams
turned into nightmares. I remember one dream in particular, in which I was going to take a bath. When I turned the
waterspouts on, fuzzy, bright colored caterpillars pushed
their way out the spout leeching onto me. I tried desperately to knock them off. I cried for help, but when my
mother would try to help me they would multiply. Finally,
my father came to my rescue. When he knocked off the
insects they would immediately die. The caterpillars had
horns and only my father could free me. I couldn't see
that, only The Father (God) could free me from the cater-

pillars (the Devil) through living water. How pitiful I had become.

> I can remember the story of the plagues of Egypt, when Moses demanded that Pharaoh let God's people go. *"He gave also their increase of caterpillars. He made a way of His anger; he spared not their souls from death. But, made His own people to go forth like sheep and led them on to safety so that they feared not."* Psalms 78:46, 50, 51, 52a (KJV)

After the death of my second child, I ran the streets even more. I stayed away from home nights at a time. I'd come home after staying out all night, only to find my husband, Larry, a faithful babysitter just smiling at me saying, "you must be awfully tired, running the street all night, trying to stay out of trouble, working everyday, and coming home to play mother and wife." But I didn't do any better. My peers repeatedly warned me that one day my husband was going to kill me.

There were other men. There were men with social status, men with money, physically attractive men and men with great personalities. Then there was Fast Eddie, as he was known, who was a little older than I was and very popular. He took to me like a magnet takes to metal. He got totally involved in my life and could afford to do so. He was married to a young beautiful lady, but I took priority in his life. We went everywhere and did everything together. All our holidays, vacations, and evenings as well as our off days were spent with each other. His wife, like my husband, grew to tolerate our relationship. We were more like buddies, than lovers. However, he was very possessive, mainly because he did not trust me.

Later, I was introduced to another man named Willie, who I liked instantly. At least I liked his personality and his happy spirit. During this period of my life, if you didn't have any money, I couldn't be bothered. But, I liked him. Aside from his best friend, I let no one know I knew him. I only saw him for intimate reasons. If he ran across me in public, I would never allude to anyone I knew him. He drank, got high on various drugs, and loved to party, not to mention he was also married. Before I go on, you can't help but think what a whore I became. Not to defend myself, but when it came to sex, I had the nerve to make a better than sincere effort not to sleep with more than one man for any period of time, because I could not use birth control. I went to the doctor a lot, took tests for venereal diseases and for pregnancy between relationships. This was the way I convinced myself that I was not quite as bad as some of the other whores I knew who walked the streets, selling sex for money or dope.

Again, I became pregnant, this time by Willie. When I confronted him, he questioned whether it was his because I was still married and I had other friends. He let me know that no one even knew I knew him. Assessing my predicament, I decided to have an abortion. Fast Eddie found out I was pregnant and wanting to believe it could possibly be his, tried to encourage me to have the baby, claiming he would buy me a house. With my insistence, one agreed to pay for my abortion while the other was to pay for my initial prenatal care. I went to the most credible underground doctor at that time, for these procedures were illegal. Because of my low blood pressure and being anemic, even after trying to build me up, he refused to take the risk. As a result, I had to use the service of a shady doctor who cared less about my health. The clinic was reasonably clean, but he seemed to be in a hurry. He packed me with gauge containing some type of solution and I was to return when I started cramping within a few days. I told Fast Eddie I was threatening a miscarriage. In his concern, he admitted to his childless wife he was having an affair with me and this was his baby.

When I returned to this doctor, he prepared me to complete the procedure. With my legs in stirrups and wide apart and a sheet covering my legs, I laid there. After a few moments, I realized he was performing oral sex. The next thing I knew, I kicked him in the head, got up from the table and left. I did abort and after a while, I had to go to another doctor for proper treatment. After this episode, Fast Eddie's wife decided to get pregnant in an effort to win his attention. Due to other circumstances, our relationship became estranged. He got involved with my sister, securing "dates" for her. Those frequent visits to his home and hanging out together soon ended.

I hadn't learned my lesson yet. I got pregnant with my fifth child in my tenth, and final year of marriage to Larry, by even another outside affair. Redd was a very good looking, hard working, and generous man who gave all his available time to me. In fact, he could hardly work for being around me. When he got paid, we would live large until all his money was spent. But there was one added problem. He was also married. His responsibility to his family became non-existent. But this time I finally felt this situation would be the straw that would break the camels' back. When I was unsuccessful in finding a doctor who would grant me an abortion because of the damage to my uterus, I decided to end my marriage. I was afraid to approach my husband like I had before. But, I had the nerve to secretly get a divorce. When he questioned the change in my physical appearance, I informed him I was pregnant, that we were divorced and that I had found him an apartment, all in one quick conversation. Again, I gave no warning or consideration for my husband's feelings. I took over all the bills we owed in an effort to justify my actions. He said nothing, but quietly moved to the address I had given him one day when I was at work. His pain showed, through the taking of everything in the house, except for the children's furniture. He did not even leave me the broom. When we did finally talk to each other, all he said was that he felt he should have had the choice of leaving me, not me divorcing him. Larry made it clear that if he could live with me as I was, I had no right to choose his destiny. However, even to this day, he remains kind, helpful and loving to both of my daughters, my son and me.

> *"Be completely humble and gentle; be patient, bearing with one another in love."*
> Ephesians 4:2 (NIV)

In my quiet time, the little I had, because I was now working full-time, I wondered what was driving me to live so carelessly. Thank God, AIDS was not heard of and that I was spared from those dreaded sexually transmitted diseases. It seemed each man had his purpose, yet none satisfied all of me. But when it is all said and done, I took responsibility for what I did. God was merciful not to let me get swallowed up in my selfish choices. I always knew God was there in my consciousness and in my spirit. [I came to realize, like a co-worker I knew of who wrote a best seller called, "Why Men Cheat", he simply explains because they want to.] We are free agents, created with the capability to make choices. No peer group, environment, or even fear can make you do something you don't want to do. [It's like one of my grand-sons who refuses to lie when questioned even to avoid conse-quences for his disobediences. If you asked him, "Why did you do it?" He simply says, "Because I wanted too."]

For some reason, we have the habit of blaming someone or something, for our actions. Yes, things and events do happen which contribute to our thought processes, but the decision is still ours. My lust for what I thought I wanted, looking for excitement I thought I needed, and refusing to ask God who made me to show my purpose only gives credence to the fact that I was just doing what I wanted to.

CHAPTER 4

No Trust

After Larry and I divorced, Redd, the father of my fifth child, a son, moved in. His drinking (although he never appeared drunk), preoccupation with me, and desertion of his family, soon got him into trouble. Had it not been for his mother-in-law's coming to her daughter's rescue, threatening to pursue legal actions, his wife would have continued to be passive and distraught over this ordeal. As a result, our living arrangement became somewhat stressed. He could not afford two families and I refused, as I mentioned before, to be second. I didn't see the advantage of him hanging around. It wasn't long before he lost his job, his family and then me.

But where did this leave me? I was paying bills from my former marriage, new ones in my current situation, pregnant and alone. Several men, new and old, came to my rescue but they really didn't have anything meaningful to offer or what

I wanted. Where I was employed, when you became pregnant you could no longer remain employed. Even though the job did foot the doctor's bills for my pregnancy I had to resign after seven months. I was still in my father's building so I didn't have to worry about being homeless. But, there was no money. Towards the end of my pregnancy I tried to abort my child or kill myself, whichever, came first. First, there was the turpentine I planned to drink. It dissolved the paper cup it was in before I had a chance to drink it. So I gave up on that idea. Second, it was the hanger and the rubber tube that I tried to put up my uterus which hurt too bad to make that effort a success. Finally, there were all those now banned prescribed pills that I decided to take, which I vomited after experiencing long moments of lifelessness. There were times when no food was in the house. Even with public aid coming to my rescue it was not enough. Soon as school was out for the summer, I sent my two daughters down south to be with my ex-husband's parents in the country.

I carried my unborn son the entire nine months, unlike any of the rest who came early. Aside from my best girlfriend, who helped me get around since I couldn't drive and was just being there for me, I was alone by choice. Because of my obsession to stay clean, I bathed in very hot water, which caused my water to break before I went into labor. Being on very good and personal terms with my doctor, he fixed it so I could collect from my insurance and from public aid to pay for my delivery and the tubule legation that followed hours later.

One day when I was taking one of my hot showers, my incision opened up. I could actually see my intestines. Being distressed and depressed, I climbed out of the tub falling to the floor screaming in a horrid rage. My ex-husband, who happened to be outside my home, rushed in and wrapped a towel around me and held me tight. I remember telling him how sorry I was for what I'd done to him only to hear him say, it was all right and I did not deserve to suffer like I did. I managed to get myself together, taking a cab with my baby to the doctor's office so he could repair my incision. I was in agony when I returned home. But, God was with me. I was almost helpless. I said a short prayer, took some pain pills, fed and changed my son, laid him on top of me, and slept for ten hours, only to awaken to find that my son was still where I put him, unharmed.

My son's father was around only for a short period. Since he lost his good paying job, he didn't have much to offer. He started driving a cab, then later became an insurance salesman and finally a bartender of all things. In trying to get child support, I found out he had fathered other children and that I was the only mother who challenged him and got child support. I had to go as far as to take DNA tests between myself, my son, and my ex-husband just to prove whom the father was. He had the audacity to deny paternity on the advice of his lawyer.

Four months after having my son, I went back to work on my previous job of four years, starting over again with a new seniority. Since I always had good work habits, I was able to return to work after only four months. Because I returned in a timely manner, I decided not to sue my employer later for parental discrimination, a legal matter that had already been filed as a class action suit and was won the following year. Between my old girl friend's mother and a Christian lady who lived across the street, my babysitting problems were of no concern. They usually kept my children all week, except for my off days, for a nominal fee. However, I still didn't make enough money to make ends meet.

So I got connected with my ex-husband's cousin. He was known for being slick. He had served time for selling mail order weapons. He looked, dressed and talked well. He was constantly looking for fast money. And I needed money. He explained how I could get bad checks cashed. Usually, I would open an account with a bad check using fake ID's and cash a lesser check on the new account. Cross-referencing was not prominent then. One warm afternoon, I was again trying to cash a counterfeit check. I felt concerned and shaky but I continued the transaction. The next thing I knew, I was detained and later arrested. Of course, I didn't have a record. Here I had a good job, children, respectable parents, and a steady boyfriend, and still did the dumb stuff. I guess I didn't look like the criminal type, because they locked me up in a cell at the end of the tier. I sat there in that chilly cell, reading all the nasty and vulgar graffiti on the wall, listening to the conversation of the detainee's as they entered their chambers for the night.

The food, I refused to eat and I refused to cry. I prayed that I didn't have to stay the entire night. I was in custody for about six hours when I was released. Somehow, a long time Christian friend of my family got in touch with her brother, who was a detective, to arrange for my release. In fact, I used to babysit his children years earlier. When the court date came, all charges were dropped. I found out that I was declared an informant for the police department. That was the end of my life of crime.

> *"My daughter you have let sinners entice you, consent not. Walk not in the way with them. Refrain from their path. For their feet run to evil, so are the ways of everyone that is greedy to gain."* Proverb 1:10, 15-16, 19 (KJV-rev.)

About one month after returning to work, I went into a local liquor store to purchase a soda only to run into Willie, whose baby I aborted approximately two years earlier. For some reason I was glad to see him. Showing that beautiful grin, he seemed to be equally glad to see me. Making small talk with him and his best friend, he mentioned that there was a young man who frequented the store who looked like my twin. At that moment this unidentified person entered the store, and it happened to be my brother. The atmosphere lessened of any hostility that was present. I reluctantly decided to invite Willie over that night. He did come over at about one o-clock in the morning and slept on the couch. When he got up the next morning to go to work he left two hundred dollars, stating he would give me more when he got paid. The next thing I knew he was there every night, eventually in my bed. Our agreement was that he would give me $250.00 every two weeks. Note my rent was only $150.00 a month.

Our relationship was very stormy. We both would party all the time and not always together. He was extremely jealous therefore accusations were always made when I came home. Physical attacks were common because he assumed that I was out having sex. Yes I would go out with other men, spend their money, and even allowed them to make every effort to encourage me to have sexual intercourse with them. But, I pride myself in not letting temptation encourage me to do what I had no intention of doing. Regardless of what Willie's insecurities were, we liked talking to each other. He loved my children and I adored his four daughters.

Yes, he was still married. I didn't object to his wife calling him concerning the kids. What I did notice is that he was beginning to stay out all night, and her phone calls were frequent. I was able to find out where she lived and her phone number. I went over to her house and left a painted note, which said, "I'm the lawnmower, and your ass is grass" down the side of his car. I went home, called her and asked to speak to him for just a moment. I made it plain to him that if he didn't return home before I went to work he wouldn't have to because everything of his would be destroyed. After a few hours, I got a neighborhood boy to put a fifty-gallon trashcan in the alley and started to burn his clothes. While I was in the closet retrieving more of his clothes, he came home. He pushed me in, and started begging and explaining. After much heated discussion, he said he would stop seeing her but he had promised to take his children to the zoo. While he was gone, I called his wife who explained that she was told that I was his landlord and he was renting a room. Since I never objected to them talking, she believed him especially since he would be moving back with her. When he returned home I confronted him. He told me quite the opposite. Our conversation must have taken longer than expected because she called. I insisted on him answering the phone. She immediately questioned what was taking him so long. She painfully had to hear that he had been lying to her and that he loved me and was going to stay with me while I listened on the other end.

We lived together for over four and half years, but separated twenty-one times during our relationship. During those times he lived out of his car for as long as a month at any given time, especially after staying out all night. It wasn't long before I realized he was getting high off of marijuana and un-prescribed pills. Then he started buying bricks of marijuana, cutting and bagging it for sale. Since the money was good, I didn't object. The parties we went to were basically pot parties. If I even looked at another man, when he got high, we fought. It usually ended up with him pushing me around and me scratching him up and then a separation. These were the times I saw other men.

I didn't want anyone for sex, just for money and

companionship. There was a married gentleman with whom I worked who had an affair while he was in the armed forces. In keeping his promise not to betray his wife's trust again, he developed a platonic friendship with me. We talked and saw each other often. He actually enjoyed his friends thinking we had an intimate relationship going on. We did spend quality time with each other. He helped me financially and took me out when he could. When Willie and I got into fights, which most times caused separations, my friend helped me get through the ordeal. He wanted intimacy without sex. It really didn't matter to me. I liked being loved, without having to make love. We remained close until Willie and I broke up for what seemed like for the last time. He decided he wanted to become an intimate part of my life, and even was willing to leave his wife. As much as I appreciated him, I didn't want him like that. Then there was Shorty. He was small in stature, country, a good provider and he had an immaculately clean looking body. Between separations, Shorty was there for me. He was stable and wanted things in life. Again, it was I. The normal expected routine was too boring. Our only excitement was when I decided repeatedly to take Willie back and his objection to it.

Besides Willie's relationship with his wife early on in our relationship, I never had any problems with another woman, just with him being so insecure in our relationship. I did creative things when he stayed out all night or came in late, like taking his clothes on the job and dumping them on the office floor. Or, when he came home very late at night I would sneak and reset the clock hours earlier and watch him hurrying not to be late for work only to find out he was actually three hours early. I even threw ice water on him and for an instant he couldn't distinguish it from the possibility of it being scalding water. He constantly stalked me while we were separated. I recall one time when he told me he was going to work, only to realize that he was hiding in the closet. Yes, he caught me on the telephone with Shorty and tried to make me eat the phone, literally. Since he lived in his car when we were not together, he often parked in front of the house for hours. At parties he actually would not let me talk or dance with anyone. He would become outraged and threaten to kill me. It was never a dull moment.

Once I gave Willie a birthday party that lasted for three days. Drugs were ever present in my house, yet I only participated once. I smoked a half of a reefer. It affected me in such a way, that when I decided to go to work, taking a commuter train, I rode for several hours beyond my stop, admiring the old buildings I passed, visualizing how they could be rehabbed. Interestingly enough, some twenty-five years later, many of these buildings have been converted into very expensive condominiums. Of course, I was late for work. After I realized what I had done, I decided I would never get high again.

I did not like losing control of my behavior but there were several times that I did get drunk and actually lost days of memory. I realized I didn't handle alcohol well. On one occasion I got drunk with my first husband while playing cards one New Year's Eve. When you lost your dealt hand, you had to take a shot of whiskey. Five fifth's later, between five players that included my first husband, sister and my two brothers-in-law, we all became incoherently drunk. Yet I had plans to go out with a close male friend. I actually used an iron board to prop myself up, all the while trying to iron so I could to go out. I still lived upstairs over my parents. On my way out I fell down the twenty-five stairs, got up, brushed myself off, and stated, "That sure was a big step."

Another time while I was out of town with a male friend I drank rum and coke, which happened to taste good. I was told it was a tropical punch. Somehow I managed to get dressed to go to a cabaret ball. During this period of my life, I found myself loving my social life with people I felt had class. Anyway, at the dance I was told I kept on dancing with virtually anyone willing to join me. After I got through each dance I sat at the nearest table and drank anyone's drink that was available. My friends actually had to escort me to my hotel room and tie me down so I would not leave. Several years later, while working, a stranger recognized me from those days, especially at that social affair. He was able to produce a magazine showing pictures of me dancing. I didn't remember this behavior or how I got home. Some three days had eluded me.

Probably the last time I got sloppy drunk was when I was visiting one of my male friend's homes. He had a management position, and was a free-lance photographer and a big time socialite. Aside from wanting me to be his escort for numerous social events, he tried to keep up with my whereabouts. Yet he paid little attention to me when I was in his company. Such was this particular evening. I found myself drinking a fifth of his expensive brandy and playing a Nancy Wilson album over and over again. He finally made me turn off the music, after which I decided to leave his home during a winter storm. I managed to make it to the corner. I sat on a snow mound and flagged down a cab. I told the driver where I lived and not to take advantage of me. Every few minutes I asked the driver to pull over so I could vomit. The next thing I knew I awakened in my bed some three days later. Larry, my first husband told me that the cab driver brought me home and rang my doorbell so someone could come and get me and so that he could be paid.

> Little did I know that not even *"drunkards, like fornicators, Idolaters, adulterers, homosexuals, abusers of themselves, or others, abusive language, extortionists, shall not be able to inherit the kingdom of God."*
> I Corinthians 6:9-10 (KJV-rev.)

All the while, when I was with Willie, I did pretty much what I wanted, especially during our many separations. I went from one adventure to another. While in college, I often took as much as nineteen credit hours in one semester and managed to stay on the dean's list, while attending school all year round. I worked eight to twelve hours a day and went out several nights a week for excitement. I took Darvon, Librium, Valium (some now banned), and sleeping pills. I took practically anything so I could keep up with my hectic schedule.

Once, coming home from work I met a good-looking distinguished insurance executive who visited my city often. We became friendly and after a while I became his mistress with no strings attached. We met at the best hotels. One particular day, while shopping in the gift shop a well-dressed man approached me and asked whom was I working for. In no uncertain terms he said I was working on his stroll and if I were to continue to be a guest I would have to cut him in. It dawned on me that he saw me as a prostitute, to make myself feel better, a call girl. It shocked me into reality. I was just a glorified whore, if that's such a person. My days for being a convenience whore were over. I disappeared out of my gentleman friend's life. The thought of being viewed as a prostitute made me sick.

I didn't realize I was thirsty for fulfillment. I was like that woman at the well. Looking for love in all the wrong places. Jesus explained to this adulterous woman, "W*hoever, drinks of the water He offers (living water of salvation), that person shall never thirst; but have everlasting life. For you have had five husband (many men) and the one you are*

with now is not yours." The truth revealed set
her free from sin. No peace outside of God.
John 4:14-18 (KJV-rev.)

To this day, I really don't know what made Willie so insecure. He often decided whom I must have been having an
affair with. One time near the end of our relationship we
picked up his brother-in-law to go somewhere. Willie had to
run an errand, leaving us alone in the car. We managed to
make small talk until he returned. After we dropped him off,
Willie questioned what we had been talking about, making
accusations. The next thing I knew, he back fisted me in my
mouth, busting my lip, which needed several stitches. I
jumped out of the car leaving my textbooks and my shoes,
that I'm was forever taking off when I'm sitting, and ran
down the street. I could hear shots ringing in my ears. He was
actually shooting at me. I knew then it was over. In all the
confrontations we had, he never hit me with his fist. He forgot
I was a woman. Ironically, he had just gotten a divorce and
we were planning to get married within the next few months.

I think he knew it was finally over. He asked me if I
would let him stay until he found somewhere else to live. I
agreed. For the next several weeks, he started accusing me of
having an affair with someone who worked with us.
Whoever this person was, I never knew him. After much
research, I got a chance to talk to the person with whom I
was being accused of having an affair and warned him about
Willie. I finally asked Willie to leave after being threatened

by him several more times. I left and went over to a friend's house a few doors away waiting for him to pack his stuff and leave. When I felt safe I returned home, only to discover my door kicked in and furniture broken. I got a restraining order. After over four and a half years, I finally gave up on him.

I often worked the midnight shift, so I could be at home with my three remaining children and go to college during the day. I managed to work and go to college full-time. In fact I completed school in three and one-half years, majoring in both Business and Secondary Education. One night I left my secured workstation to call home from a public phone when I saw Willie approaching me. For only an instant I was actually glad to see him as three months had passed since I last saw him. Suddenly fear gripped me. I tried to quickly return to my secured workstation. But I couldn't quite make it. Without saying a word, he grabbed at me and I proceeded to defend myself. I felt a severe pain between my legs and for a few minutes, I was not conscious of anything. Finally the pain brought me back to reality. He had kicked me. He quickly left and I was alone. Shortly afterward, a co-worker showed up and helped me decide what and how to deal with my dilemma. I had to contact one of my friends to come and take me to the hospital. I stayed there for about a week, recovering from a ruptured bladder. Strangely enough Willie's ex-wife called me and told me that he said he wished he had killed me, then no one could have me. As much as I wanted to, for personal reasons, I decided not to prosecute him for assault. For fear of me doing so, I felt I didn't have to worry about Willie bothering me anymore because he did not know what kind of trouble he might have gotten into. If I had pressed charges for assault or attempted murder, we both would have lost our jobs.

It's funny how you convince yourself you love someone and just one act of disrespect can change your whole outlook about that person. Shortly after I recovered from my injury Willie's mother died. Somehow I felt obligated to support him during his bereavement after he finally called me. When I was in his presence and a few times thereafter, I couldn't make myself consider him my lover, even after he tried desperately to get me to forgive him and to resume our relationship. I forgave him, but I no longer wanted him. It was over. I could not forget that he had forgotten I was a woman. It has been over twenty-five years since I've seen him. Sadly, I found out that he finally lost his job of twenty-four years, due to drugs.

God's words call us to be free. *"But, do not let your freedom indulge the sinful nature; rather serve one another in love. The law of God summed up in a single command: Love your neighbor as yourself (even in forgiveness without hatred). For if you keep on biting and devouring each other, watch out or you will be destroyed by each other."* Galatians 5:13-15 (NIV)

It's interesting that I actually wanted to settle down with Willie. For some reason it was becoming important to me not to keep on living in sin, shacking. I felt like I was living beneath my privilege. The success of the marriage wasn't important, it was the feeling that I am necessary, worth having, and the security of belonging. This is not to ignore that I paid my dues in caring and putting up with him. My soul was still not satisfied. A good man wasn't good enough. An obsessed man who I believed loved me abused me. It was my choice. I was like a ball in tall grass, I couldn't see around, only the heavens when I looked up. Regardless of what someone thought of me or I of myself, something inside of me wanted to be respected as well as loved.

CHAPTER 5

A Family Affair

Even with making some bad choices trying to satisfy the need for excitement, I was still responsible to my family. My Christian parents were naive about some of the things my two sisters went through during their young adult lives. I felt it was necessary to get involved. Regardless of my own situations, I wanted them not to be corrupted by what the world had to offer even in my sinful state. I always wanted the best for everyone. Like me, all of my siblings got married soon after their eighteenth birthdays. Only one of us is still married to their first spouse. However, our second marriages have survived.

After my middle sister's marriage ended in divorce she met John who she eventually lived with. Our youngest sister kept her son most of the time while she was working as a nursing aide. I started noticing that regardless of how hot it got outside she still wore a sweater. One particular day I came home early from work. She was supposedly watching our youngest sister's and my kids. I surprisingly found her in the kitchen cutting heroin. When she looked up at me, she asked me with an air of arrogance, "what are you looking at?" In a quick instant, I found myself swiping the fine white powder, the needle and the spoon off the kitchen table. She got hysterical and cursed me while trying to salvage what she could. I guess I lost it. I told the kids to go next door. When she could not get the drugs up, she tried to leave. I immediately went upstairs, got a gun and made it clear to her that I would kill her rather than to let the drugs do it. I actually locked her inside the house. Her boyfriend, stood outside the door begging me to let her go. In my anger, I realized he must be responsible for what had happened to her and I shot through the door. Someone ran to the next block to get my brother. He was still at work, but his wife called him, and then he called my sister and me. My sister answered the phone, explaining to him I was keeping her against her will. She told him to reason with me. While he was talking to me, my sister made an effort to open the door. As she tried to rush past me, the next thing I knew, I began beating her across the head with the phone receiver while my brother was on the other end of the line screaming to get our attention. Blood was gushing out of her head and running down her face. The entire neighborhood had gathered around, trying to get me to open the door. Finally, I let a few friends in to help my sister. Someone called my father and the police. I waited on the porch, watching my father, who chose to park down the street instead of in front of the house. For the first time in my life, I saw my father being reluctant to deal with such an ordeal. When the police arrived I explained what had happened. When they tried to assist my sister, they found heroin stuffed down in her bra. In their best judgment, they decided to arrest her for possession of a controlled substance. They transferred her to the hospital where she got over forty stitches. While we waited, the doctor informed us that she had over two hundred track marks on her body, including some on her back. We left knowing none of our lives would be the same.

The court put her in the custody of my father. Meanwhile, we as a family, after getting over the shock of this ordeal, decided that we were going to force her to go cold turkey into withdrawal. With the support of her caseworker, we would stay with her around the clock. I watched her sweat, vomit, get cold chills, scream, and shake for hours at a time. We had to keep her confined. Everyone took turns watching her on an eight-hour shift. She often begged us to let her go because she was too weak to force her way out. Once she called the police telling them she was being held against her will. After we explained what we were trying to do, they encouraged us and left. We were handling our responsibility for about three days. Then it was our older brother's turn to watch my sister. He had the night shift. She somehow talked him into taking her outside for a walk and a smoke. Walking to a busy corner, he decided to use a public phone. While he was not focusing on her, she quickly got into someone's car and was gone. We didn't see her for several months. Even before this incident, I knew she was stealing clothes from elite stores. After a short while, she claimed she and her boyfriend had to leave town in a hurry for several years to secure better jobs. I found out later that she was stealing prescription pills and selling them on the black market. Since she had disappeared, my parents were permitted to gain custody of her son.

When she did return to town she only came around when she was broke, begging for a handout. She was tall, had beautiful skin, hair, teeth, and hands. Her body was well kept except for how she dressed. But, as time went on she got obese and dirty. One time while she was visiting our parents, her eight-year-old son found her in the bathroom half naked on the toilet with a needle stuck in her arm and passed out. In a panic my mother called me. She was coming around when I got there. In my anger, I threatened her and told her not to ever come around our parents again.

The next time I saw her was when she came to my home some time during the night. I was still living on the second floor of my parent's building, with my children's bedroom located in the front of the house on the other side of the living room wall. I was awakened during the night by a foul smell. I noticed that my living room lights were on. I followed the smell, which was coming from where she was sitting on the couch, which was located along the wall that separated the living room from the children bedroom. As I walked across the floor, water in the rug was squishing between my toes. My sister was in a nodding posture with a cigarette that had extended ashes sagging between her fingers. She raised her head just long enough to tell me to go back to bed and that she had everything under control. I snatched her up from the seat, only to notice that she was sitting on a burnt hole in my couch. Once again I went ballistic. The neighborhood was awakened as I ranted and raved over the fact my children's lives were in jeopardy. My best girlfriend's mother came to calm me down. In viewing the situation, she stressed the need to emerge my couch cushion in a tub full of water. In carrying out her instructions, I was shocked when I saw the cushion go up in flames after over an hour later. Usually, when I'm very upset, I stay busy to maintain my composure. I often catch up on my ironing. My sister didn't leave well enough alone. Cussing, she complained that it was no big deal because no one got hurt. As she spoke, I saw the hot iron becoming a weapon, like the telephone receiver once was. My boyfriend stopped me. Once again, I told her not to come around her family, again.

Months had past when my mother's sister came to visit us. We decided to have a family picnic. She wanted to see my sister. It was a gruesome search, going into a drug-infested community, asking for her. It was obvious she was prostituting because of the cars that stopped and tried to pick me up thinking I was her. When she saw me, she was irritated because I was spoiling her score. After I explained why I was looking for her she decided to show up. Her short visit consisted of begging for money, supposedly to buy much-needed shoes. Of course she didn't buy any.

A few months later she was arrested and mandated to get some help in a drug abuse program. There she met and married an ex-drug addict who was then a counselor. They were both thrown out of the Center for breaking the house rules. They ended up living with his mother. One night, while her husband was hospitalized someone, whom I believe knew her, robbed her while she was in her car in front of her home. Her mother-in-law discovered her after she heard my sister's car but not hear her coming into the house. She was found dead from a gunshot wound to the back of her head.

My parents were unable to deal with her death and gave me full responsibility to bury her. If it were not for my second husband, Ronnie (who I will introduce later) who helped me with the arrangements by using his cousin, a funeral director, this ordeal would have been even more stressful. The only request our parents made was that the service be held at the funeral home since she didn't go to Church and that my parents pastor's eulogy would make no reference to my sister. He was to preach salvation to those sinners; her so called friends, which would be attending her funeral. Meanwhile, her husband never recovered from his illness and died a short time later. My sister was killed at the age of thirty. Her killer was never found.

My sister never appeared to have a God consciousness, even though as a child she went to church. She never realized that the

"Wages of sin is death, but the gift of God is eternal life." Romans 6:23a (NIV)

She was eternally lost.

My youngest sister on the other hand, was always there for me. She was a cute tomboy while growing up. But, she fell in love at the early age of fifteen and she was soon pregnant because we were never taught sex education. My mother (a minister) and father (a deacon) were truly embarrassed. They sent her to live with our relatives in another state. There she would continue her education and have the baby, who was to be adopted by my parents or at least that was the plan. When her daughter was born she refused to give her up and returned home only to get pregnant again by her daughter's father. As soon as they both became of age they got married.

When our parents relocated, buying another building close by, my sister moved into their old apartment. I continued to live on the second floor over my sister. Since she was a homemaker, she kept my children. She was an excellent caregiver. The children had fun all the time and their Christmases and birthdays were grand events. Because they went to a Catholic school, they all were exposed to many cultural events and activities unlike myself. They were living a sheltered, but wholesome life while I continued to run the streets.

This sister's husband had a drinking problem. He always had a decent job, but when he got drunk he was obnoxious and even violent. Profanity became his first language. They often had bid whist parties and what started out to be a fun evening would often turn into a fight between them, especially if they were losing. He would even attack her for no apparent reason. One day when I was in their apartment he came in starting a fight. I jumped in and stabbed him with a serving fork to help her defend herself. When I proceeded to leave, he threw his TV at me while the children were watching it. Electricity was flying everywhere. He wasn't finished yet. The next thing I knew, he was shooting his gun up through the ceiling, I guess to injure me. He gave up and went into a drunken sleep, only to wake up in good spirits as if nothing had happen.

One particular day, my sister was cooking greens for the entire household in a thirteen-gallon canning pot. Her husband had been out all night drinking. He came in behind her without saying a word and hit her with his fist in her kidney area. With one swift motion and with both of her bare hands she grabbed the boiling pot, raised it over her shoulder and she emptied the pot of greens on him as the pain gripped her body. He screamed in pain as he fell to the floor. He suffered from second and third degree burns down his right arm, neck and chest area. She suffered no injuries. He was hospitalized for several weeks.

Meanwhile, she and her kids were immediately relocated out of harms way, for we did not know what he would do when he got out of the hospital. They never got back together again. The marriage ended in a divorce with a restraining order. A short while later, her ex-husband's best friend introduced my sister to a co-worker of his at a New-Year's party. He was a widower with four children of his own that were not much younger than my sister. They got married after a short courtship and relocated to California, remaining happily married for over thirty years until his sudden death.

> *"Praise to our God and Father of our Lord Jesus Christ the Father of compassion and the God of all comfort, who comforts us in all our troubles, so that we can comfort those in any trouble with the comfort we ourselves have received from God."* II Corinthians 1:3-4 (NIV)

My little sister received comfort from God and her family and let it overflow to a new family, a struggling widower with his children, loving him until his death. His children continue to cherish her as their mother.

In our growing up, all my brothers, as well as my sister and I, picked up the spirit of hard work from our parents. Each one of my brothers picked up one of my father's professional trades; a certified interior decorator, licensed barber, and an owner of a printing shop. Even though we all have a God consciousness, knowing how to live a Christian life according to the message of God's word and the example our parents lived before us, only two of us worship God as my parents did. Today, we are all productive citizens living quiet lives.

As we grew older, we saw very little of each other. We seemed to have our own agenda, coming together mainly to address concerns of our parents in their later years. Being the oldest, I was given the responsibility of managing their affairs. I had never seen my parents show any visible sign of affection between them during most of my life. Yet in their later years, they demonstrated a tenderness and patient display of love and care that was unlike anything I've ever seen between two married people. My father exemplified the kind of love God shows for us in love for my mother who suffered from dementia in her eighties.

Growing up with my illness and my desire for adult male relationships made for a limited childhood. After my relationship had ended with Willie I was determined to finish school. My neighbors were my babysitters and I used unique methods to instill in my children the values of responsibility, trustworthiness and love for each other. They could not go out much, but they could have all the company they wanted where I could watch them. I learned early that I must be consistent in my childrearing and have effective communication. Even though I was seldom at home, I managed to spend quality time with my children, mostly on Saturday mornings when my three children would pile up in my bed with me, talking, playing, polishing my nails, combing my hair, sometimes even while I slept. I kept a scoreboard that monitored the duties they performed and their conduct. This was to avoid daily ridicule or punishments. The good they did would erase the bad. As a result, they got far less spankings. However, I was creative in their punishments, like when they forgot their schoolbooks. I would make them hold heavy books for as long as I deemed necessary, which encouraged them not to leave them at school. I wanted them to understand that there are consequences for being neglectful and disobedient. This was a relevant response that would have a lasting effect. It worked.

Today, my three children are married and have pursued their college educations. One of my daughters has earned her Ph.D., another is a registered nurse, and my son has a secured job while being self-employed, after leaving the armed forces as a certified chef. Each one of my children has confessed Christ in their lives. All of my grandchildren are in gifted academic programs. I must admit, I'm blessed by God and give Him all the glory. With sincere gratitude for the grace of God, I was spared from the consequences of my sins and thus far there has been no generational curse on my kids. Even though one of my children suffers from chronic Lupus, she thanks God every day for life. I used to tell my children there were three things I must do as their parent: (1) buy tennis shoes, blue jeans and a tee shirt; (2) feed them oatmeal for breakfast, peanut & jelly for lunch, and (3) give them lots of love. The rest of the things and stuff they wanted they could work and get for themselves.

Over the years, I found out that God would give you what you need if you give your soul to Him and are obedient to His word. He will even give you some of the things you want. He has done so for me. God has given us a family to love and bond with. Our lives often are intertwined so we can support, love, and influence each other. We as sinners are often affected by our experiences in our relationships. Satan knows the importance of destroying the family. Thank God for the institution of our natural family.

CHAPTER 6

A Vision Revealed

Before I met my present husband and after Willie was finally out of my life, I had casual relationships with other men. Some male friends were constant throughout my adult years. I had two new friends who took up some of my time when I wasn't working full time or going to undergraduate school full time. This interval lasted for a period of nine months. One gentleman took care of my social and financial needs, while the other was more suitable as a friend and companion. I didn't care that they knew about each other and my children's fathers. None of them could please me enough for me to be concerned about their feelings for me. All that mattered was that they all treated me right. The physical intimacy I craved proved to be unfulfilling and made me feel incomplete as a worthwhile person of character. I was growing tired of feeling empty. While I felt good about my academic accomplishments and my relationship with my children, I hated myself for the lifestyle I had chosen to secure the happiness I felt man could give me. I had no peace. I had drama for excitement but no peace.

I wouldn't give up on the idea that having a man in my life was essential to my happiness. I would assess each potential prospect, making it clear to them what their roles in my life were, and that they were not the one. I sometimes had dreams about a certain man, the same man, but he never had a face. One day when I was picking up some encyclopedias that had fallen on the basement floor, I noticed a warrior on a horse. When I looked closely, I observed it was a handsome Mongolian with a Fu Man-chu mustache. From that point on, my dream had a face. A short time later, my life was changed forever after. Before then, I was looking for love in all the wrong places. I liked being loved, but never having to love.

> *"I denied myself nothing my eyes desired. I refused my heart no pleasure. My heart took delight in all my work, and this was the reward for my labor. When I surveyed all that my hands had done and what I toiled to achieve, everything was meaningless, a chasing after wind; nothing was gained under the sun. Then I turned my thoughts to consider wisdom, and also madness and folly."*
> Ecclesiastes 2:10-12 (NIV)

At the end of one workday, returning to headquarters where I check-off from duty via a commuter train, I noticed this young man who obviously worked for the same company. He was the man, the very man I had seen in my dreams. I wondered why I had never seen him before. For the next ten minutes I watched him closely not believing my eyes. Then it was over, at least for a time. I made up in my mind that I had to meet him. But, how! I decided to get in touch with one of the popular co-worker's to see if she could find out who he was. After a detailed description, she knew it was Ronnie, better known as Mad Mac. The good news was that she knew he was not married. For the next three weeks, I caught the same train looking for him, but no Ronnie. Finally, I approached the motorman and asked about this mysterious individual by name, only to find out that it was his scheduled route, but he took off a lot. So, I began to lose hope of meeting him. The following week he was back on his job. There he was and I was not going to let another opportunity pass me by. I decided to introduce myself. When I nervously approached him, he addressed me by my name. Being startled, like a little girl I found myself saying, "How do you know my name"? Then he said," that's not all I know about you." You see, when I saw him he must have also seen me. When we got to the end of our tour of duty, I asked him if he lived in the direction I was going. He asked, "Why?" I told him I wanted a ride home. He said he had planned to take me home anyway.

While driving home from work, Ronnie told me how he

found out who I was. In his explanation, I realized that his friends were some of the same persons with whom I to associated, including my present boyfriend who was one of his best friends. For one moment, this awareness gave me doubts of the possibility of any involved relationship for we both had moral principles concerning interfering with our friends personal relationships. Somehow, neither of us let this situation keep us from getting to know each other better. We talked for five hours while parked in front of my house. Our hearts poured out to each other as we discussed what we wanted out of life. Tears came to my eyes as I told him of the failures with some of my relationships with men, the desire to be restored in love and acceptance with my parents; my wanting to have a successful marriage based on love and togetherness; and my desire to be a Christian family in serving God. I explained how dissatisfied I was with my past lifestyle. He was receptive, gentle, and concerned. He expressed his needs and experiences with his past marriages. Ronnie was living with a very wealthy, young lady. His smallest wish was her greatest desire. He found nothing really wrong with her other than her choking love for him. She was extremely possessive and insecure. Ronnie was as drawn to me as I was to him. He decided during those few hours that we belonged with each other; so much so, that he proposed marriage to me that very same night. At first, I took the proposal as a flattering gesture of caring and an attempt to impress me after knowing my feelings concerning marriage. But, when he actually started discussing plans as to what immediate preparation had to be made to make this a reality, I became frightened. I knew if he carried out this plan, I would have taken the risk of becoming his wife without knowing anything about him. I felt positive that he was a gift from God and I wanted him.

> *"My daughter, preserve sound judgment and discernment, do not let them out of your sight; they will be life for you. Then you will go on your way in safety, and your foot will not be afraid; when you lie down, your sleep will be sweet."* Proverbs 3:21-24 (NIV-rev.)

I thought my dream might have finally been becoming a reality, finding a perfect man. Maybe, I had found someone who would love me in spite of what I was; someone who understood what I could become; someone who believed in family life; someone who could fix anything like my father; someone who could protect me; someone who would provide for me; someone I could please; someone who could make me feel good and good about myself; and someone who could give me joy. Does this man exist or is this what I need for my sin sick soul? Is he the man or am I looking for God Himself? I've got to have him and I need him. But, who is he?

Ronnie confessed that he was in the process of getting a divorce. I was somewhat relieved, for without using any logical reasoning I would have gotten married for the sport of it. However, he assured me as soon as his divorce was final we were getting married.

The excitement of this meeting left me in ecstasy. Not once did it enter into my mind after he proposed that he was making flattering remarks to get next to me. The challenge of a new relationship gave me hope within myself. His conversation made me know that we wanted the same things in life. I had finally met the man I had long been dreaming of and praying for. I even took the time out to thank God for His goodness. For all good things come from Him.

The next day the excitement was still fresh within my soul. I shared the details of my meeting with Ronnie to my children and my best friend. Before the next morning was over, Ronnie called stating that he told his lady friend about having met me, and that he wanted to share his life with me. He made preparation to move in with his sister until we could get together. To my surprise, he had called my boyfriend to inform him of our meeting and his intention towards me. This, I must say was quite unusual. I admitted we had met but denied the seriousness of the relationship, for in reality I had no idea of his devotion to my family or me. Other than a general rundown of his past, I knew very little, or next to nothing of his obligations and commitments to it, nor did he know anything about mine.

For the next few weeks he visited sporadically. When he did visit, friends that we both worked with accompanied him most of the time. He never announced his visits. He just showed up. The times I tried to contact him by phone were always unsuccessful. His grandmother, who was senile, only identified me as being Ronnie's lady friend. When I called his sister, she was uncooperative for she could not see the logic in our relationship. To her, her brother was giving up so much for so little. Because of Ronnie's girlfriend's frantic reaction toward the termination of their relationship, he decided to return to their home, hoping to end his affair with less complication.

In my excitement over this new man in my life I shared the details of my dreams and conversations with Ronnie to my mother, who had been estranged from me for about fifteen years. The point I wanted to share with her was that if he were all that he said he was, and all the things he wanted to be, salvation for me would be possible. Our conversation lasted over three hours. This particular night my mother and I shared our feelings, likes, dislikes and hopes. We had never conversed as much as we did that night. I will say, up to this point, not knowing what the future had in store for me, if I never got anymore out of this relationship with Ronnie, I found a renewed bonding with my mother. I became aware of the love and concern she had for me; she was praying for me; she grieved over the years for me, especially when I ran away from home. She actually feared for my sanity. She knew of the battle of conviction within my rebellious spirit. She long since recognized those different moments when I desperately wanted to be loved and to love someone; wanting to be faithful and truly honest with myself and everyone around me. It sickened my mother when she heard me speak with authority of myself as being the devil's advocate. She saw how I could ignore and leave my children with someone, mainly their father or my sister, for days at a time, yet had a possessive love for them. She heard how inconsiderate I could be when breaking up others' marriages, knowing full well that I didn't want the man on a permanent bases. My mother knew how cruel I could be when I spoke the hurting truth without sympathy or even being tactful. Yet, she had seen me speak out against injustice. She was aware how I detested professed Christians who were hypocrites. She noticed my deep-rooted attachment to my children and the idolized endearment I felt for my father. My mother knew I was under a state of spiritual conviction, refusing to give in until I got whom I wanted to share my earthly life with. Her love for me was overwhelming, all of which was shared along with tears. She so much wanted me to know God before it was too late. She was grateful for God's blessings that I was receiving. Never in all her life had she ever heard my voice ring with so much anticipation and excitement. If I believed in Ronnie, she also believed in the promises of him being a permanent part of my life.

A few weeks after I met Ronnie, the Friday after Thanksgiving, I had to enter the hospital to have a hysterectomy. The surgery was a success. I didn't have a chance to let Ronnie know about the details. In desperation, I had my girlfriend find out where he lived. Then she sent a telegram to his home, that said, "Help", signed MD. After about two nights in the hospital, I had a dream. I dreamed that I was dying and all my family and friends were summoned to my bedside. But, I refused to die because Ronnie wasn't there. When he finally arrived, I woke up. My body was cold with slimy sweat and I stank like something dead. I called for the nurse. The smell even made her sick. She helped me into the shower and cleaned me up. The next day I had several visitors. One was an old boyfriend. By early afternoon Ronnie arrived with flowers. I immediately dismissed my friend for my new company. He said he figured that the telegram came from me and he called my children to find out my whereabouts. He said he was just stopping by because he had to go to work. But, he actually stayed with me the entire evening instead of going to work.

Ronnie met my mother by phone. He conversed with her as if he had known her for years. His interest in religion impressed her. She, like the children and I, fell in love with him. He expressed his love and his intentions regarding me. I had already given her a summary of his past. All she could say in response to talking to him and listening to me was regardless of what I might have to go through, wait on him. She also believed in the words that he had spoken especially his desire to be a Christian.

"The Lord searched me and knew me. He knew when I sat and when I rose; he perceived my thoughts afar off. He discerned my going out and my lying down; He's familiar with all

my ways. Such acknowledgement is too wonderful to attain." Psalms 139:1-3, 6 (KJV)

My mother, knowing this same God, grabbed hold to my dream. My children adored Ronnie. The very possibility of his visit put them in a frenzy of excitement. The few times we talked he mapped out our future. Yet, I saw no evidence, only promises of his intentions. He went so far as to say that he was my messiah, who came to save me from myself, giving me life. I would look upon his bearded face as a god or sometimes wonder if he was the devil in sheep's clothing. I could almost visualize a halo around his head. His plans were my dreams. I became frightened whether I was worthy of him for he often expressed his moral concepts. With a childhood of extreme poverty; motherless at the age of two; a father confined to a mental institution; raised by a mean abusive grandmother; two unsuccessful marriages which ended in the acts of infidelity on the part of his wives; and having fathered a son afflicted with a birth defect, he survived admirably. Yet, he was more than willing to get involved again with me. I told him I had lived a wild permissive life, having conceived my children out-of-wedlock and through adultery. Now I was not able to have any more children, which I knew he wanted. However nothing seemed to curtail his interest in me.

King Solomon, the greatest and riches king, because of his request for wisdom from God, expressed his Love for a slave girl, loving her more then all his other wives and concubines. He fell in love with her at first sight. Like him, I realized that *"his love was mine, and I was his; as he browses among the lilies. Until, the day breaks and the shadows flee, I turn to my lover, who is like warrior of a stallion on rugged hills. All night long in my bed I looked for my hearts loves; I looked for him and did not find him. Scarcely, had I passed them, while I found the one my hearts loves. I held unto him and would not let him go until I had brought him to my mother's house".* Ronnie, like Solomon, let me know *"I had stolen his heart with one glance of my eyes. Pleasing is my love and the fragrance of my perfume more than any spice. I was a garden locked up, my sister and soon to be a bride; a spring enclosed a sealed a sealed fountain."* You see I had yet to become intimate. Song of Solomon 3:1-14, 4:9, 12 (NIV)

Whenever we went out for an evening of entertainment, we frequented the very places I went with my other friends. Ronnie's peers took a dim view at what they felt was a triangle with his best friend and myself. However, Ronnie was bold and greatly feared by his peers. He feared no man. Therefore, no one challenged our relationship. His countenance was so positive and assuring, I felt that I was in the company of the most desirable and bravest man alive. Several times I was in the company of both Ronnie and our friend. They had several confrontations about me. Even though they wanted me to make up my mind as to which I preferred as a mate, I tried to avoid making that decision. Ronnie, with full control over the matter felt confident because his friend was already married, even though he was willing to leave his wife in order not to lose me. I knew I had to have Ronnie, however I did not want to be presumptuous. My reservation was that I could not depend on Ronnie nor did I want to altogether relinquish the peaceful affair I did have with his friend. Ronnie talked much but gave up nothing. He had little respect for my past lifestyle. I had no effective way to contact him, especially since he had returned home to his girlfriend. However, his unorthodox behavior only enhanced my interest in him. On the other hand, my friends felt I was in some state of depression (since I was recovering from a hormone altering surgery) and bored because I was not working and couldn't go to school. Referring to the old cliché, it was obvious that my nose was wide open, wide enough to drive a locomotive train through it.

"My lover is mine and I am his; he browses among the lilies (other women) until the day breaks and the shadows flee. Turn my lover, and be like a gazelle (African antelope who

*are noted for their lustrous eyes) or like a
young stag (unbroken stallion) on the rugged
hills."* Song of Solomon 2:16-17 (NIV)

God had let my fantasy become a reality. My determination to find the man of my dreams distorted my judgment that God Himself the maker of the dream was whom I needed. This sinner's soul gave way to my flesh senses, yet inwardly I wanted to please God, the giver of the gift. I had met what I believed to be my soul mate. God had answered this sinner's prayer. I was ignorant to the fact that God made me for Him.

CHAPTER 7

Desire Of The Heart

From the first week in December, Ronnie came over to my house whenever the mood struck him. He even made promises that he would help me financially for Christmas, since I was temporarily off from work. When he did come to visit he would entertain my children and the neighboring children for hours at a time. The kids adored him and I was convinced he was the one. The closer it came to Christmas, the less of him I saw. I eventually resorted to some of my old boyfriends for support. The holiday was a big thing in our household and I wasn't about to spoil my children's Christmas. He finally came with a couple hundred dollars and a tree on Christmas Eve. I believe he was surprised that I managed to get along without his help since I already had a tree and my children's Christmas in place.

I didn't see Ronnie for the rest of the week. I couldn't get in touch with him. By midweek I had reestablished my casual relationship with my ex-boyfriend. A couple of weeks earlier, they had met up at a lounge, got drunk and then returned to my house waking my children and me. With me in their midst they demanded that I choose between them. Ronnie's argument was that my boyfriend was married and could not satisfy my needs. I refused to respond to the childish gripes and demands. The commotion led to a fight or should I say a scuffle that continued into the snow-covered street. My children witnessed the entire episode from inside and found the entire ordeal entertaining.

Early on New Year's Eve, I was relaxing in my bed with my boyfriend watching TV when the doorbell rang. The children ran to tell me that Ronnie was coming upstairs and bringing someone with him. Before I could get out of the bed he appeared. To my surprise he brought his two children with him. He introduced me to his five-year-old son who was born with Down syndrome and his stepdaughter who he raised from his second marriage. That was not all. He brought lots of his clothes with him. He announced that he was moving in and that my boyfriend had to take everything in my house belonging to him and get out. My friend said he couldn't take his belongings home when his wife was home, so he had to come back and get them some other time. Ronnie requested that I put on some street clothes and go with him. We dropped off our friend and Ronnie's children at their respective homes. Next, he took me to his only sister's home and his childhood girlfriend's homes and introduced me as his future wife. We returned to my home where he spent the night. When he woke up the next morning, he simply mentioned that this was not right way to leave his girlfriend and he must go. But when he returned, he said it would be for good. He said his goodbyes and left. I found out later he never told his girlfriend he was leaving.

For the next twenty-one days I didn't see or hear from him. The very day I was considering letting the same ex-boyfriend (Ronnie's friend) visit me, Ronnie made his appearance again. This time he brought all his clothes, boxes and two fifty-five gallon fish tanks. Without his asking, I allowed him to move in with me on a permanent basis. Mind you we had yet to become intimate. However, I refused to unpack his boxes. I felt he was subject to wake up the next morning or any morning and leave again.

During the next month we went out a lot, frequenting the same lounge. What I began to notice about Ronnie was he would get drunk which caused him to be sick and unable to work for a couple of days at a time. He was well liked on his job and was one of the most sociable persons I'd ever known.

One particular day, my daughter's friend called me from the corner store to inform me that a lady was asking for and looking for me. Not only that, she had pulled a gun on her thinking she might have been me. She left several hours later after having no success in finding out where I lived. Ronnie found out later that it was his ex-girlfriend. Then she decided to announce to him she was pregnant. She even made an attempt to commit suicide. She finally realized that nothing she did or said got his attention. Ronnie got tired of her badgering him on his job and leaving messages with his sister. One Tuesday after we had lived together for about 20 days, Ronnie asked me to marry him as soon as possible. Two days later, Thursday, February 26, 1976, we were married.

I had a fantasy of getting married one summer day on the beach at sunrise, followed by a picnic reception. I would wear a long yellow chiffon dress with a large straw hat and be barefoot in the sand. Now we had to plan a quick marriage ceremony because I was not going to get married at the Court House. Our off days were Wednesday and Thursday. That Wednesday, we notified our immediate family, contacted a minister (a co-worker), asked our best friends to be our witness, applied for our licenses after taking a three hour blood test, purchased matching rings and suits, and made arrangements to use my parents house (without their knowledge) to perform the ceremony. Then came Thursday.

We took my parents to a very popular restaurant, where Ronnie asked my father for my hand in marriage. My father had no objections since we were shacking already, plus he knew that I was going to do what I wanted anyway. When we brought them home they noticed that there were lots of cars on their property. They were confused about what was going on. When they entered their home, they saw a house full of family members and some friends. My four-year-old son kept trying to tell them we were getting married. After waiting a couple of hours for my best friend to show up, we exchanged our vows while the O'Jays softly sang "Stairway to Heaven". We had a cake and champagne in celebration. Later that evening we went to our favorite hang out. The best house drinks lined the bar in our honor. Ronnie tried to drink most of it.

The man I ordered from God was finally mine. At least I thought he was. Let me explain. A couple of days later I decided to unpack the rest of Ronnie's clothes and other personal items. I came across his divorce papers and decided to read it line for line. When I got to the last page, I noticed that there were no signatures and no seal. To double-check, I looked for my divorce decree and reviewed the last page which was properly signed by all concerned. I showed Ronnie the discrepancy. He immediately called his lawyer, who explained that those papers were mailed to him for approval and signature in order to finalize the divorce. In other words, he was still married to his second wife; He was a bigamist. Ronnie demanded that whatever correction needed to be made it had to be done immediately. We had to wait two weeks before it could be finalized because the judge was on vacation. So on March 12, 1976, during our lunch hour, we secured our divorce papers and sought a judge to waive our waiting period so we could reapply for another marriage license. We got remarried that evening in the home of another co-worker who was a minister of the gospel. The celebration was on again with plenty of drinking and dancing. That next night, we were out again and came home about two o'clock in the morning. We went to bed as soon as we got home.

About five o'clock that morning, I was awakened because I heard Ronnie talking to someone. He was sitting at the foot of the bed. When I sat up, I asked who he was talking to? I noticed there was an indention in the bed as if someone was sitting next to Ronnie. When he turned to explain whom he was talking to, the indention flattened out as if someone had gotten up, but I saw no one. Then Ronnie said, "If we were going to have a successful marriage, we would have to change our lives." Apprehension filled my very soul. I wanted to understand exactly what he was talking about. He made it clear; we needed to go to Church and become Christians. I couldn't believe what I was hearing. The man that I was convinced was a gift from God wanted to give God his life. I asked him if he knew where he wanted to go to Church and if he understood how to become a Christian. In sober sincerity, he said he would do whatever it took. He agreed we would attend my parent's Church where my mother was a minister and the new members' Sunday school teacher and my father was a deacon. I asked if he wanted to give his heart to God. He said he did. We got on our knees in that small bedroom and we gave our hearts to God, asking Him to forgive us of our sins. We spent the rest of the morning talking, waiting until we could go to Church to give our testimonies.

"Have mercy on me, O God, according to your unfailing love; according to your great

compassion, blot out my transgressions. Wash away all my iniquity and cleanse me from my sin. For I know my transgressions, and my sin is always before me. I have sinned against you and did evil in your sight, so that you are proved right when you speak and justified when you judge. Surely, I was sinful from birth, sinful from the time my mother conceived me. Surely, you desire truth in the inner parts; you taught me wisdom in the inmost place. Cleanse me with mint leaves. Wash me and I will be whiter than snow. Let me hear joy and gladness; let the bones you have crushed rejoice. Hide your face from my sins and blot out all my iniquity. Create in me a pure heart, O God, and renew a steadfast spirit within me. Do not cast me from your presence or take your Holy Spirit from me. Restore to me the joy of your salvation, and grant me a willing spirit to sustain me." Psalms 51:1-12 (NIV)

Early that morning, we got ready for Church, wearing the outfits we got married in, since we didn't have any "Sunday-go-to-meeting clothes". We had to use public transportation to get to church. The car Ronnie had, I found out was bought by his ex-girlfriend and she had it repossessed. When we walked in during the Sunday school hour and my mother saw us, she rejoiced for she knew in her spirit that something wonderful was about to take place.

I want to pause here for a moment. This is just a reflection of what it must have been like for my parents, especially my mother as she watched me drift away from the covering of God's presence. It was at this stage of completing the last few pages of this book, some twenty-five years later since I penned my introduction, a revelation became evident. Recently, one Sunday morning during our morning service, where my husband is now pastor, a time is allowed for the congregation at large to make publicly known any prayer requests for all to pray about. A concerned mother stood up and begged for the saints to pray earnestly for her young daughter who was raised up in the Church, sheltered, well provided for, and loved by both parents in the home like I was. Her daughter, who knew God, had turned her back on Him, seeking the lust of the flesh for gratification, which had proven to be unfulfilling. She was looking for love in all the wrong places. Yet, when things didn't go her way or hard times confronted her, she cried for mercy from her parents and the Church family. But what stuck with me was the mother's urgent heart wrenching plea. It dawned on me for the first time how my mother must have cried out, asking God to have mercy on me, the sinner. I can imagine my mother begging God with free flowing tears, to give me a little more time. She surrendered me to His will, wanting Him to get my attention but not to kill me. As I prayed with this mother who feared for the loss of her daughter's soul, I felt a glimpse of my mother's pain. I know it had to be so because I have seen since then, more than a few times, my mother's tears of joy seeing my life turned around. I thank God for salvation and her memories of my changed life for she remembers no more. My mother suffered from Alzheimer's disease before going home to be with God.

Like I said, we were just waiting for the appropriate time to announce our visitations with God to the entire congregation. After the preached word, the pastor gave an altar call, which was our opportunity for our testimony. I introduced my new husband, who then had a distinctive hairstyle, long mustache and side burns. He looked like a slick version of the movie character Shaft. We explained our conversion and desire to worship there at the Church of God, the church in which I was raised. God had answered my ultimate desires…Salvation for my husband and me.

> Like Jesus said to his friends and neighbors, *"Rejoice with me; I have found the lost sheep. I tell you that in the same way there will be more rejoicing in Heaven over one sinner who repents than over ninety-nine righteous persons who do not need to repent."* Luke 15:5b-7 (NIV)

The saints and I knew the angels in heaven rejoiced in our decision to give our lives to Christ.

I was not in the mood to go the work that afternoon, but

I went. However, I was late. When I got there, I had to see the shift superintendent. I didn't know whether he understood or not but I explained what had just taken place that morning. He listened carefully to my every word. Then he asked me what Church I joined. When I told him which one, he told me that he thought that it was the same kind of church his wife was raised in. He gave me his name and his wife's maiden name. And sure enough I knew her from years' back. What was intended to be a disciplinary hearing turned out to be a reunion. Of course no charges were issued. I was given that day off as a vacation day. God had truly answered all my prayers.

> *"Ask and it will be given to you, seek and you will find, knock and the door (your heart) will be opened to your salvation which is free for the asking."* Matthew 7:7 (NIV)

God is good. I, the sinner have the man and God. I have a second chance at a life of spiritual and physical love. I was truly grateful. I have it all. I have wonderful children, an education, God, and a perfect man. I appreciated God, but I founded myself worshipping the man. I actually felt I could live this Christian life now.

CHAPTER 8

Not The End, But A New Beginning

When I defected from the devil's army, he tried to make me wish I hadn't given my heart to God. I felt he decided to devote all of his time to making me sorry for my decision to become a Christian. Let me explain what I mean. I made it clear to God that if he gave me what I wanted, I would serve him for the rest of my life. The first draft of this book was completed some twenty-five years later. Circumstances and consequences made it difficult and awkward to pen these words. I would start and stop. What has taken place in our lives since then is another book in itself. The first and foremost serious mistake I made was putting my husband before God. Now that I had a good looking, fun loving, hard working, and Christian family man, I felt I had it all. What was worse was I made him feel he was all that, plus a coke, chips and the tee shirt.

Everything I did and felt was predicated on his wishes. My life became his. I believed I was what I was, because of him not God. His God gifted charisma made him very popular with his new church friends as it had with those with whom he partied. But God wasn't having that. It wasn't about Ronnie it was about me, for God is a jealous God.

I wanted to write about my meeting, the relationship, and our marriage and shared salvation with Ronnie. It was like a fairy tale. I was eager to share my first penned words with him soon after we got married. As he read the first few pages, he physically got sick, even vomited when he realized he had married a whore. I had slept with men and co-workers he knew. He made me feel so ashamed; I hid those tattered tear stained pages. The episode was so traumatic for him. He considered quitting his job and leaving me. I was so distraught about his reaction I couldn't work. My mother called me and sensed something was seriously wrong and asked me to have him to call her. I lay helpless in my bed, believing as quick as I had gotten married, I would be getting a divorce becoming his third ex-wife. My past had come back to haunt me. The reaping what you sow had become a reality. My past, hurting other men's women, being candid about my relationships, bringing other men's babies into my ex-husband's home without remorse, extorting money for simple pleasure, and humiliating my parents began crushing my consciousness. Yes, in the past I did what I wanted. Now, when I took a good look at the things I had done and how it affected those I care about, I began to realize the seriousness of my actions. My flesh had dictated to my soul's emotion, will and desires. But, my God's consciousness took preeminence over my life. I had to put these things behind me. That was then and this is now. I'm a new creature.

> *"Therefore, if anyone is in Christ, he is a new creation; the old person is gone, the new has come."* II Corinthians 5:17 (NIV)

Yet, the very thing I felt I needed to walk this Christian walk was leaving me. I had a choice to trust God or rely on a man. I chose GOD. As I groaned in my suffering the words of prayer escaped me, but a peace came over me. Clear beautiful voices were singing in my ears, "Do you know where I'm going? I'm going up yonder". In my spirit, I knew I would be all right. God gives and He takes away. Blessed be His name. As confirmation for my faith in trusting, accepting and believing in God, the phone rang with Ronnie's voice on the other end telling me he was coming home.

> *"Sing to the Lord, you saints of God, Praise His Holy name. For God's anger lasts only a moment, but his favor lasts a lifetime; weeping may remain for a night, but rejoicing comes in the morning."* Psalms 30:4-5 (NIV)

He explained later that my mother, the woman who once gave up on me, let him know with the authority of God that what I did was then and this was now, for my sins were under the blood (forgiven).

I was so grateful that he didn't walk out on me. I only looked up to him all the more. I can think of an old church song I heard as far back as when I was a child. This song became life to me. "I'll never forget the day God spoke to my troubles, those words of peace that made my burdens go. He broke the chain that bound me and set all my joy bells ringing, praise to God's majestic Name."

God allowed Satan to attack me first, but since I did not lose hope he started in on Ronnie. His poor work habits started to affect our well-being. His secured job was in jeopardy. I took the liberty of writing to his superior a letter explaining some of Ronnie's issues, his changed life and that he was now married and more responsible. This letter, I believe made an impression and saved his job since I was such a credible employee.

Ronnie quickly got involved in Church ministry. He got his calling to ministry approximately two years later. Like many young men he let his guard down and fell to ungodly indiscretions among our peers. It was made clear that Ronnie was not perfect. To handle the humiliation I witnessed and the pain I felt, I convinced myself I was reaping what I sowed. Ronnie's honesty, humility, repentance, and obedience to his spiritual discipline left me no choice but to accept his apology. Since then, in spite of our growth in the Lord we have not always been subject to the Holy Spirit. We've both disappointed God and each other. But through it all we continue to hold on to each other and God. If we have learned nothing else, it is that without God we are nothing, can do nothing, can be nothing. Twenty-eight years later, in spite of us, we have had successful careers (now retired), attained educational goals, grown in the ministry, and are now responsible for other souls. My husband serves as pastor and I as the church administrator just thirty miles from my sordid past.

God's goodness: A call to Salvation

I look back now knowing that God's grace and mercy exists when we are in our sins, giving us space and time to come to ourselves like the prodigal son who left his father's house, living large and sinking to the gutter only to realize even as a servant he would be better off returning home. God, like a father, received him wholeheartedly and restored him to his rightful place. But on the other hand you take a risk as to how long God's Spirit will convict you to repentance. No day is promised to you so let today be the day of your salvation. Once you acknowledge that you were born a sinner (whether you are a good or bad person), and with humble and sincere repentance ask Him (Jesus) for forgiveness and believe that He is the son of the living God who died for your sins, He is faithful to forgive you. After you openly acknowledge that you have given your heart to God, it takes time, determination and a desire to please Him, like you once did for yourself. I'm talking about a change in your lifestyle. You must develop a new attitude of righteousness as you surrender your entire being, mind and heart in obedience to God's Holy Word and as you allow God's Spirit to take preeminence over your soul.

Know this that *"Salvation is found in no one else, for there is no other name (Jesus) under the heaven given to men in whom we must be saved."* Acts 4:12 (NIV)

I was raised to know God's ways, which makes me more accountable than those persons who never knew Him. Yet, I turned to seek pleasure of the flesh. As I now know, the lust of the eyes and flesh and the pride of life is Satan's weapon to destroy your very soul. I put so much effort into and took so many risks trying to find that which could satisfy my soul, yet never found true peace. Somewhere deep down in my soul, I didn't like what I was becoming and who I was affecting. With the prayer of my loved ones and the training in the way of God, I came to know that "sinners have souls too". God is faithful to forgive. Today there is peace and joy in my soul, brighter than the perfect day for God has given me His Spirit and He wants the world to hear it. Everyday I want to walk close to Him. I asked Him to grant me this, for I am still maturing into His Likeness, and desirous that He continuously keep me from all wrong.

"Seek first His kingdom (his will) and His righteousness (his ways), and all these things

*(even that certain man) will be given to you
as well."* Matthew 6:33 (NIV)

Why is it so important to me to make my story known?
You need to know, that everything that you say or do, the
choices you make, the situations you may find yourself in,
and your treatment of people along the way affects who and
what you will become. As you look back over your life, you
may see some of yourself in me. Some of you are not as bad
and some are much worse than I. Whatever way you
honestly see yourself, God can make a difference in your
life. Your past mistakes and failures, now victories in Christ,
can become the road for someone else's salvation.

My mother's favorite song comes to mind. "If I can help
somebody as I pass along. If I can cheer somebody with a
word or a song. If I can show somebody who's traveling
wrong. Then my living will not be in vain. If I can point
somebody to the lamb (Jesus) once slain. If I can tell somebody that He rose again. He can cleanse the guilt and wash
the stain. Then my living will not be in vain." My life has
become purpose driven in doing God's will as His servant
so I may die in peace like my parents and receive God's
promise of eternal life with Him.

"To God be the Glory for the things He has done for me."
The End for a new beginning in Christ Jesus.